CW00556675

STOUR VALLEY RAILWAY

THROUGH TIME

Andy T. Wallis

AMBERLEY PUBLISHING

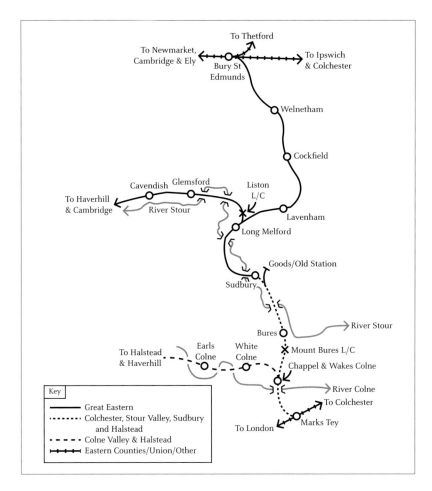

To all Stour Valley and Great Eastern people, past, present and future.

First published 2011

Amberley Publishing
The Hill, Stroud
Gloucestershire, GL5 4EP

www.amberley-books.com

Copyright © Andy T. Wallis, 2011

The right of Andy T. Wallis to be identified as the
Author of this work has been asserted in accordance
with the Copyrights, Designs and Patents Act 1988.

ISBN 978 1 4456 0472 5

British Library Cataloguing in Publication Data.
A catalogue record for this book is available from
the British Library.

Typeset in 9.5pt on 12pt Celeste.
Typesetting by Amberley Publishing.
Printed in the UK.

Contents

Introduction

The former Colchester, Stour Valley, Sudbury & Halstead Railway was authorised by Act of Parliament, in 1846, to build two lines: the first from Colchester to the Hythe, and the second from Marks Tey to Sudbury, with a branch to Halstead. The second line was duly completed in 1849, and opened with intermediate stations at Chappel and Bures. The branch to Halstead was duly forgotten about due to lack of finance.

Further extensions were authorised in 1847, from Sudbury to Long Melford and Long Melford to Lavenham, but never got off the ground due to lack of money. Two further Acts authorised extensions from Lavenham to Bury St Edmunds, and the second authorised the lease of the CSVS&H Railway with the Ipswich and Bury St Edmunds Railway. The CSVS&H Railway was formally leased to the Eastern Union Railway in 1848, and in turn was leased to the Eastern Counties Railway in 1854, when they took over the running of the EUR.

The Eastern Counties Railway now controlled or leased the majority of lines in its area and, together with the other principal railways in East Anglia, was amalgamated into the Great Eastern Railway in August 1862. This included revised powers to build an extension from Sudbury to Shelford via Long Melford, Clare and Haverhill, and a branch from Long Melford to Bury St Edmunds. The new lines were opened 9 August 1865, which included a new station at Sudbury.

Under the Great Eastern Railway, the fortunes of the line reached their zenith by the earlier part of the twentieth century. The Great Eastern Railway passed into the new London & North Eastern Railway on 1 January 1923, and the new owners started a cost-saving programme that saw the closure of duplicate signal boxes on the line and reduction of the single-line sections, and also included upgrading of the final sections to token working.

During the late 1920s and 1930s, special summer excursion trains ran from the Midlands and Cambridge, via both the Stour Valley and Colne Valley lines, to Clacton and Walton. Traffic over the line peaked again during the war years, and for a short time afterwards passenger traffic was heavy – especially during the period after the war when petrol rationing was in force.

From 1 January 1959, steam traction was replaced by diesel locomotive-hauled trains for both freight and excursion traffic. Local services were worked by DMUs and Rail Buses. Unfortunately, this did not slow down the losses being made over the line. Costs were closely examined and plans to withdraw passenger services over the Bury branch were proposed and duly implemented on and from the 10 April 1961. The last passenger service to travel over the whole line took place in June 1961 when the Ramblers' Special worked from Liverpool Street to Bury St Edmunds via Marks Tey and Long Melford. Freight continued to run as far as Lavenham from the Bury end of the line. The section from Lavenham to Long Melford was lifted in 1962. Freight on the Bury line finally ceased in April 1965.

Following publication of the Beeching Report in 1963, British Railways published plans to close the whole line between Shelford and Marks Tey in April 1965. There was strong opposition to the closure plans, principally led by the local authorities. In August 1965, there was a public hearing held at Sudbury into the closure where all objections were heard. The decision of the meeting was published in November 1965 and the line north of Sudbury, through Haverhill to Shelford, was doomed. However, the line between Marks Tey and Sudbury was reprieved. As all the local authorities had objected to the closure, British Rail demanded a subsidy of £26,000 to keep the line open for another year; they later raised the figure to £52,000 in January 1967. As this was not forthcoming, the line north of Sudbury closed completely on 6 March 1967. The last trains ran on Saturday 4 March, and freight had already been finally withdrawn from the line in October 1966.

This book will show you what has happened to the stations on the line over the last forty-four years, since closure of the route north of Sudbury, together with the surviving branch from Marks Tey. Also included, a look at the East Anglian Railway Museum at Chappel and Wakes Colne.

ATW
April 2011

Marks Tey

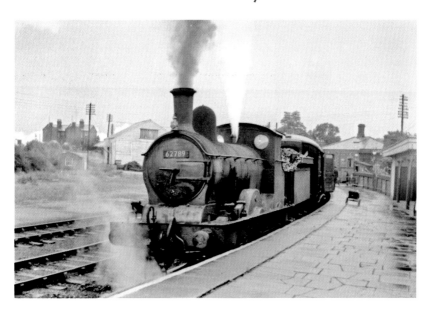

Locomotive 62789 ex-LNER class E4. These 2-4-0 tender engines were in their final days, being of GER origin. It is seen blowing off steam at the Marks Tey branch platform, whilst waiting for departure time with a down working over the line on a wet August day in 1956. To the right of the locomotive is the goods yard, with the goods shed in the background. (Brian Pask) Today, this view is still available, although the branch platform has been shortened. The former goods yard is now a car park, and the old goods shed is in industrial use. The platform building in the background is still in use as a waiting room, staff accommodation and toilets. (Paul Lemon)

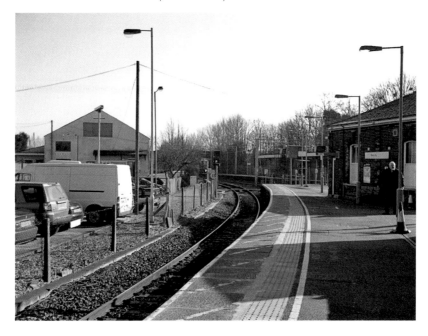

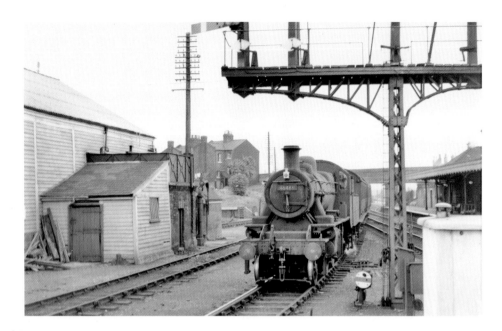

Ivatt-designed class 2MT passes under the splendid four-doll signal to enter the Marks Tey branch platform with the 17.34 Clacton–Cambridge via Halstead service train, 21 July 1956. These services usually loaded to eight coaches and were well-patronised during the summer holidays. (Leslie Robert Freeman/Transport Treasury)

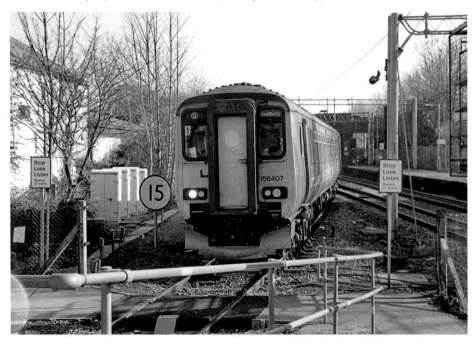

Class 156 Diesel Multiple Unit arrives from Colchester with a Sudbury-bound train. For most of the day, the unit shuttles back and forth between Sudbury and Marks Tey. The old goods shed can still be seen on the left; however, the old station cottages seen in the top picture have been demolished. (Paul Lemon)

Right: Brush Type 2 diesel locomotive number D5537 (later designated class 31) stands at Marks Tey. With the return working of the Ramblers' Special, which was the last train to fully travel over the whole of the Long Melford to Bury St Edmunds on 4 June 1961, the regular passenger service had been withdrawn from the Bury branch two months previously. (Brian Pask)

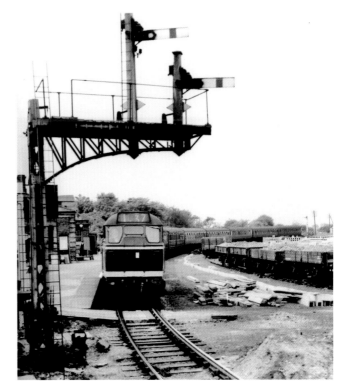

Below: The same view today would have meant standing in the middle of the track, so instead the view is from the up main platform, showing the branch platform and car park. The branch platform has been cut back to just two coach-lengths. (Paul Lemon)

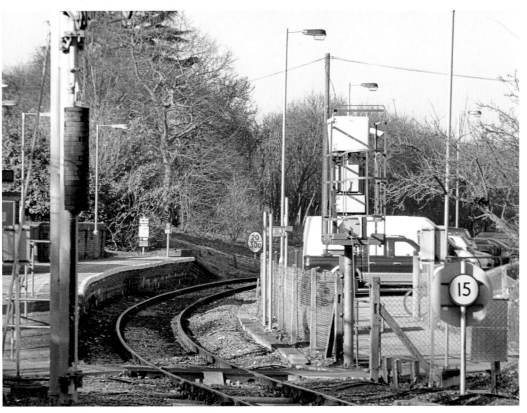

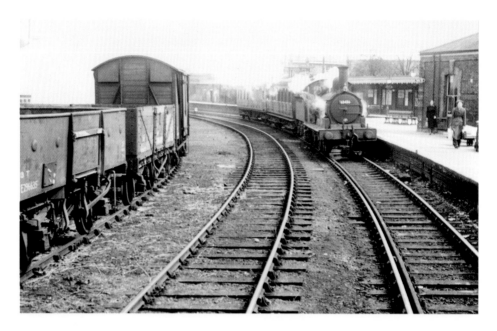

Above, ex-GER locomotive, classified class J15 by the LNER number 65456, is at Marks Tey on the 12.00 passenger train to Haverhill via the Colne Valley line, 6 May 1955. The goods yard, with some trucks and vans, can be seen to the right. (R. M. Casserley) Due to ongoing rebuilding works at the station using the end of the car park, it was not possible to exactly reproduce the first view. However, we see a local up main service train formed by a class 321 electric unit arriving. All the old station buildings have gone from the up platform, with the exception of the canopy. (Paul Lemon)

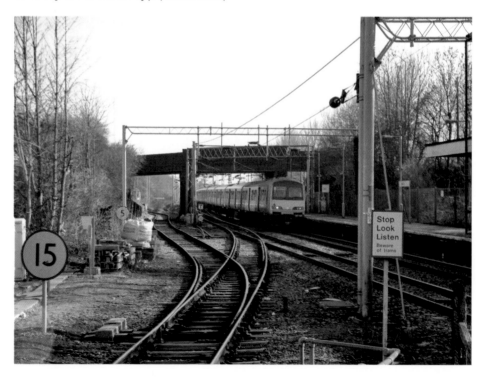

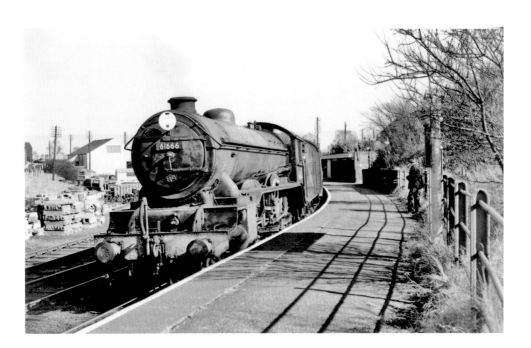

LNER class B17/6 locomotive number 61666, named *Nottingham Forest*, at the head of a down service via the Stour Valley line, waiting for departure time at the Marks Tey branch platform, 23 March 1959. By this time, it seems that the goods yard is being used as storage for S&T concrete troughing – no doubt used on the ongoing main line re-signalling. (Chris Gammel) This part of the branch platform has long since been demolished, so by leaning over the car park fence you can get a similar view looking back at the station. The bank on the right used to be the platform. (Paul Lemon)

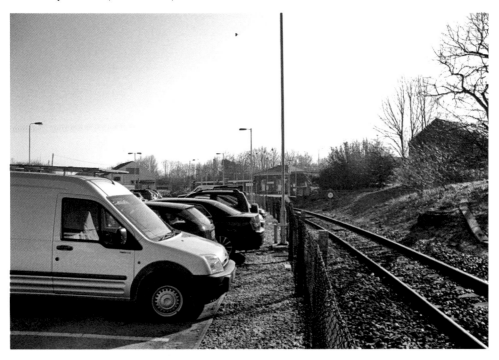

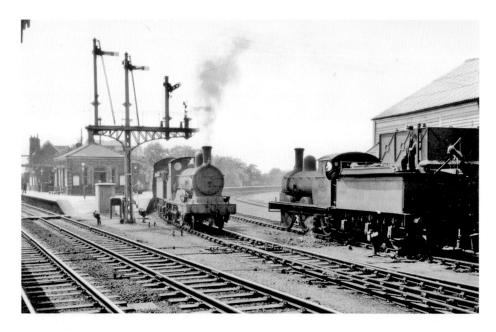

Ex-GER locomotives 62794 and 65456 are seen at Marks Tey station, 1 August 1955. The 62794 is signalled for the main line to Colchester, and awaits departure with its passenger train. Meanwhile, the 65456 is being serviced, with the fireman pulling forward the coal in the tender whilst watering the locomotive at the same time. (Brian Connell) Today, the view is of the short branch platform and the car park. The track on the right of this view leads to an engineer's siding. All other track has been removed, and the land has been given over to car parking. (Paul Lemon)

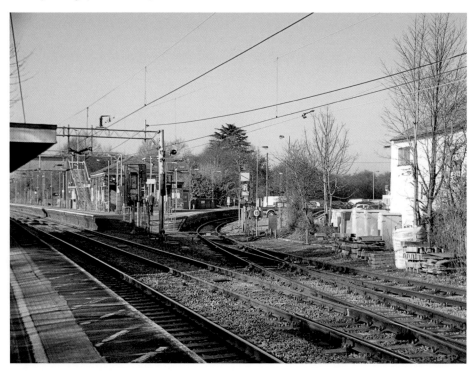

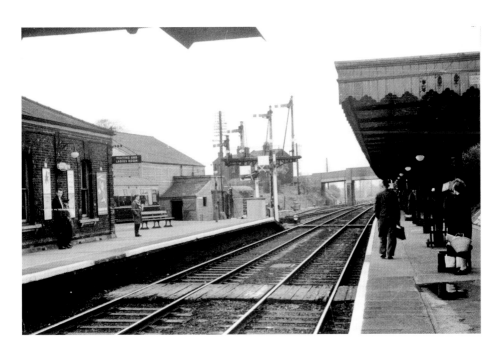

A view from the up platform towards the down and branch platforms, taken in 1961, prior to the resignalling of the station. The building on the down platform still stands today, however the splendid semaphore signal is long gone. (Stations UK) Today, the area is dominated by the overhead power lines, but the station building and old goods shed are clearly still visible. The up main canopy has been shortened over the years. (Paul Lemon)

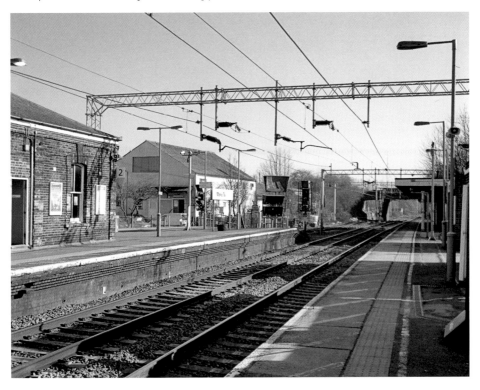

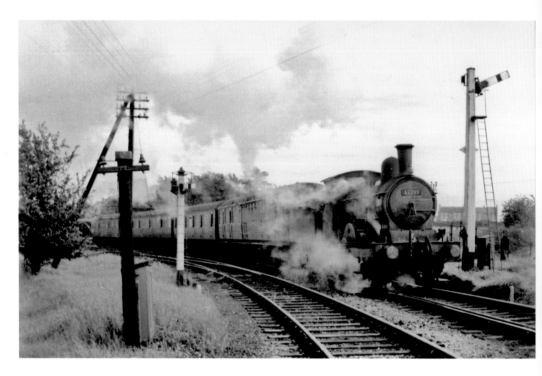

Above, ex-LNER class E4 locomotive No. 62789 departing from Marks Tey station on a down local passenger working, 25 August 1956. The line in the foreground was the connection off the single line into the goods yard, long gone as the goods yard is now a car park for commuters. (Brian Pask) Below is a contrasting view of a modern diesel working on an engineer's train, passing through Bures Station, 18 July 2005. (Ray Bishop)

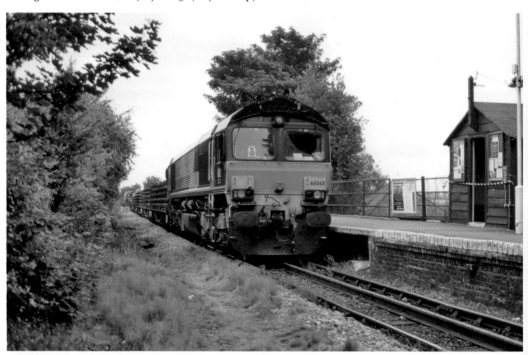

Chappel & Wakes Colne

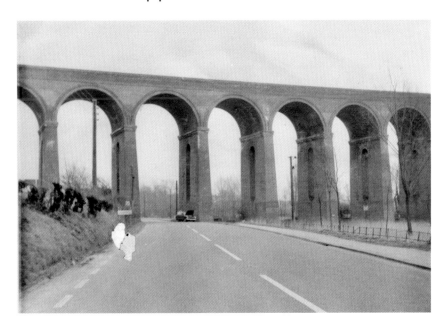

Close-up of Chappel Viaduct, which carried the line over the Colne Valley and the adjacent road – the A604, now A1124. This view was taken in 1968; note the lack of traffic on the main road. At that time, the A604 was the main route from Harwich and Colchester to the Midlands via Cambridge. The viaduct – the longest in East Anglia – took 7,000,000 bricks to construct. It and was opened with the line in 1849. (Dickie Pearce) Today, this magnificent structure still carries trains over the valley, and in recent years has seen large sums of money spent on it to keep it in good condition. (Paul Lemon)

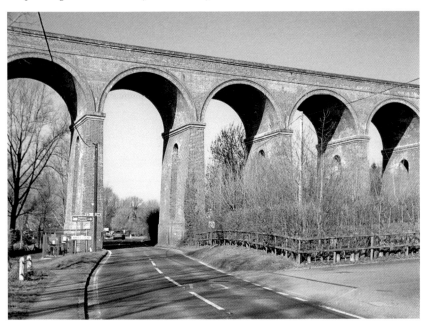

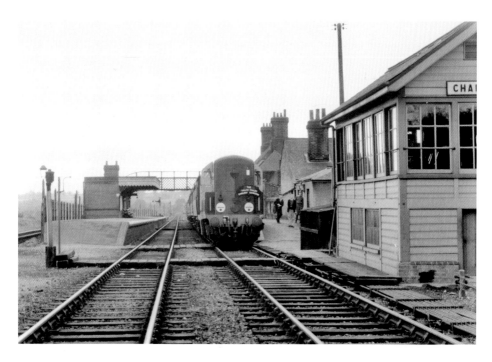

Type 1 diesel D8236 (later designated class 15) stands at Chappel & Wakes Colne station, awaiting its return as a private excursion to Halstead on 8 October 1961. This was the last excursion over the Colne Valley metals, as the passenger service was due to be withdrawn 1 January 1962. (A. E. Bennett/Transport Treasury) Below, taken from a slightly different angle, the main buildings at Chappel are still in use by the railway museum. The up platform buildings were demolished by BR long ago. (Paul Lemon)

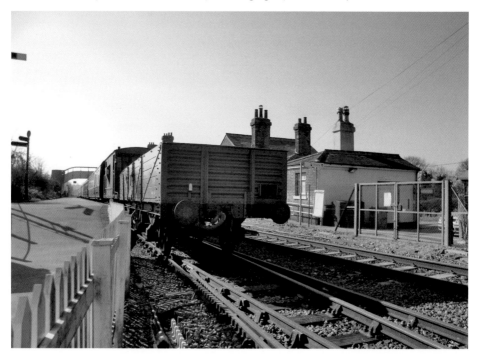

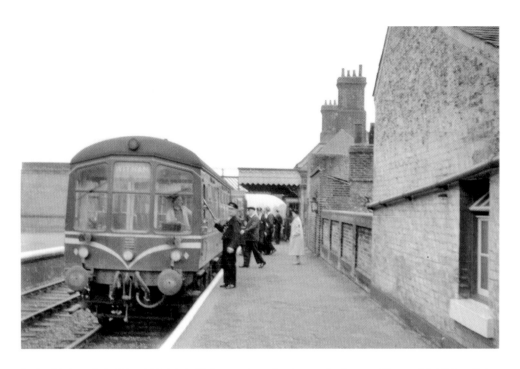

Derby Lightweight Diesel Multiple Unit stands at the down platform at Chappel & Wakes Colne station, awaiting departure to Cambridge via Halstead and Haverhill, despite the destination blind saying Witham! The single line section to Earls Colne was controlled by the large electric train staff, which can be seen being handed over to the driver of the DMU. (Malcolm Root) Today, the platform has been shortened and narrowed into a footpath. The building on the right still stands, albeit with a different window style. (Paul Lemon)

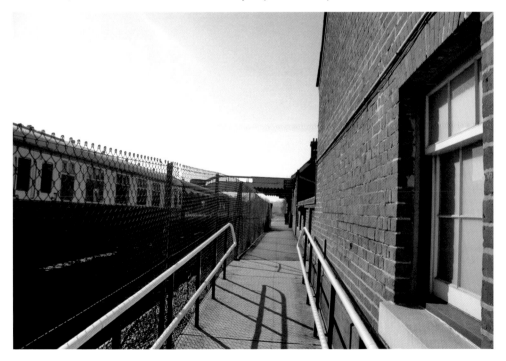

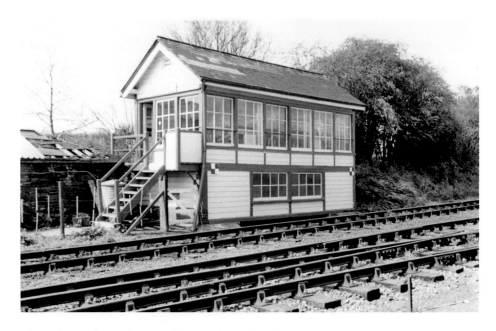

Chappel & Wakes Colne signal box, still standing but not in use; it now forms part of the East Anglian Railway Museum. The lever frame was restored to the building after being removed by BR for scrap extra parts coming from the former signal box at Braintree. The signal box opened in 1889, and contained a thirty-eight-lever Saxby & Farmer lever frame, later extended to forty-two levers. The box finally closed, together with the crossing loop, on 20 August 1967. (AAD758/Historical Model Railway Society) The box, resplendent in green and white paint, is now open to visitors as part of the Railway Museum. (Paul Lemon)

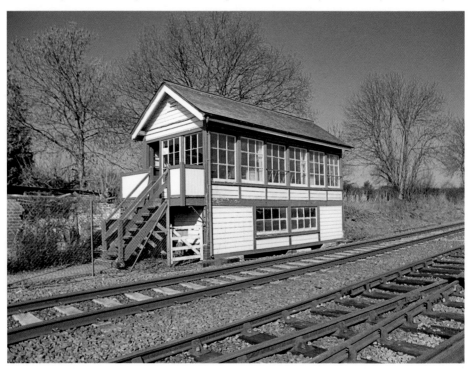

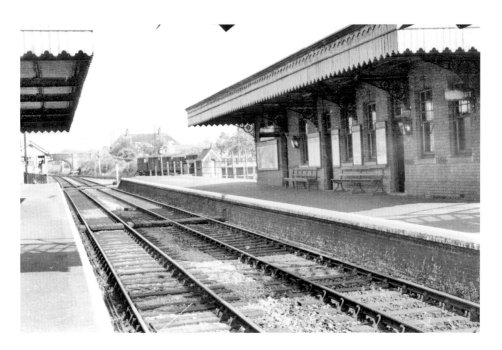

General view of Chappel & Wakes Colne station, taken from the down platform looking north with the original up side buildings, signal box and goods yard all visible, in 1959. Over the next few years, plenty of changes would take place to this view. (Stations UK) Today, the branch line is restricted to the left-hand pair of rails, and everything else is part of the railway museum. Unfortunately, the buildings on the right were demolished by BR in the 1960s. (Paul Lemon)

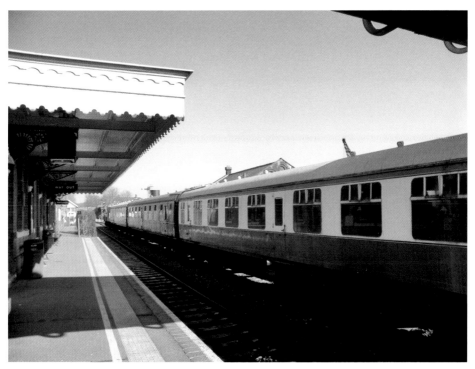

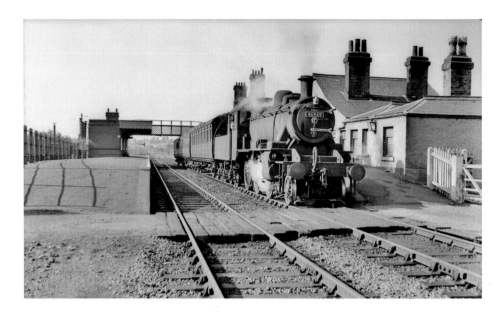

Above, 2MT Ivatt-designed locomotive No. 46469, newly delivered to Colchester, stands at Marks Tey station with a down working over the Colne Valley line to Haverhill, 25 August 1952. The running of separate trains over the Colne and Stour Valley lines was quite common after 1944, although the practice of splitting and joining still took place at Chappel & Wakes Colne well into the mid-1950s. (Gerald Sivior) Today, turning through 180 degrees, we see the local branch line service passing Chappel signal box en route to Sudbury. The track in the foreground is the EARM connection with Network Rail, controlled from the Museum Ground Frame, which is out of sight behind the train. (Paul Lemon)

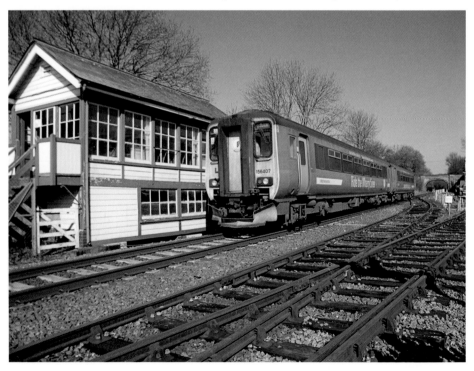

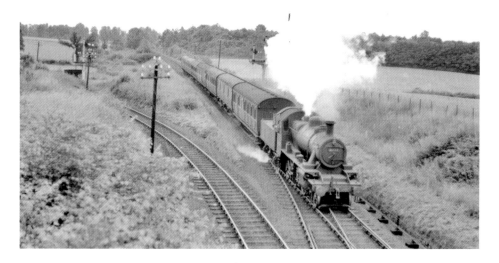

Ivatt-designed class 2MT No. 464xx passes Chappel Junction on an up direction local passenger service for Colchester during the 1950s. The line merging on the left is the Colne Valley branch. Sometimes a connection was made at Chappel & Wakes Colne station, but from 1944 it was usual practice to run separate trains to Marks Tey and Colchester rather than join or divide them at Chappel. (Dr I. C. Allen/Transport Treasury) The line is seen climbing steeply out of the Colne Valley. The track panels on the left are on the site of the former junction. In fifty-plus years, much tree growth has taken place. (Paul Lemon)

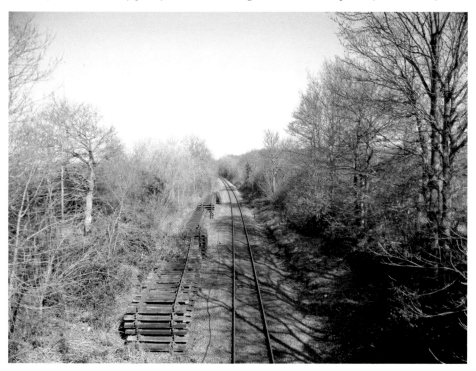

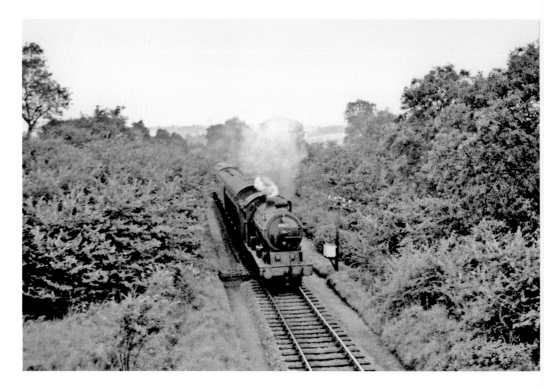

Locomotive 64673, near Mount Bures level crossing, on an up local passenger working, 16 August 1957. The level crossing at Mount Bures was manual gates until the mid-1990s, and was protected by working distant signals. (Brian Pask) A two-car DMU climbing towards the summit of the line at Mount Bures Level Crossing. This view was taken in 1994, before the level crossing was modernised and converted to an Automatic Barrier Crossing. (Paul Lemon)

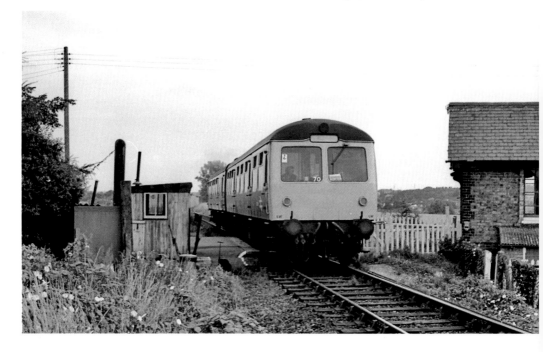

Bures

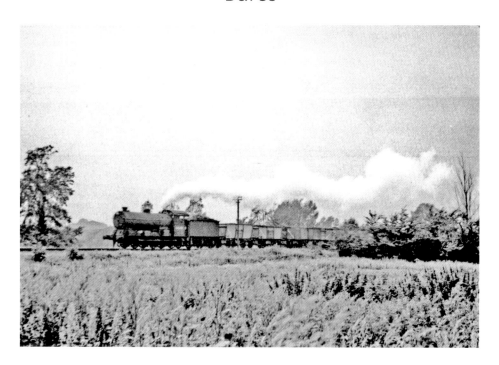

Unidentified J19 locomotive on a goods working near Bures, 16 August 1957. After departing from Bures station, the line drops down into the valley of the River Stour, which it then follows until Sturmer station. (Brian Pask) Today, there is no steam, but a similar view is taken of the local branch service train north of Bures station, proceeding towards Sudbury. (Paul Lemon)

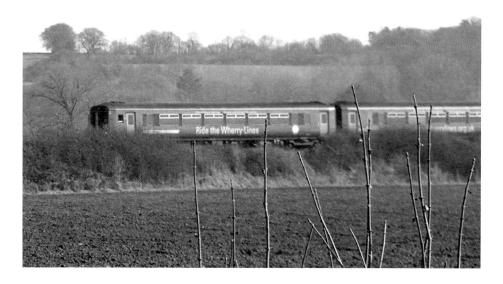

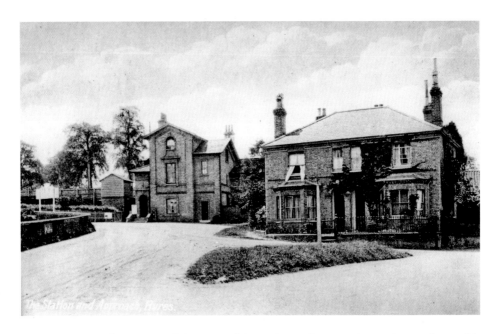

Great Eastern Railway view of the original CSVS&H Railway station at Bures, along with the two station cottages, taken from the main access road. This building incorporated the Station Master's house, and had three floors, the platform being reached by stairs to the first floor. The station buildings were demolished in 1973, leaving a small wooden waiting shelter for the use of waiting passengers. (Lens of Sutton Association) The station buildings have been long demolished. The area in front of the station is now a small car park, and the station cottages are now private dwellings, whilst the former goods yard has been given over to houses. (Paul Lemon)

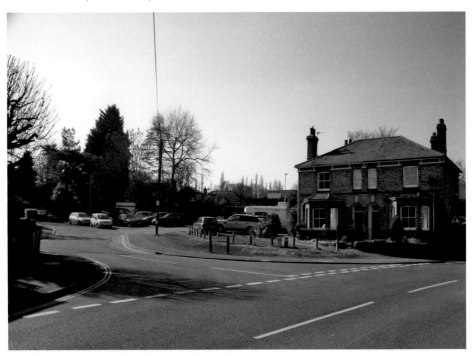

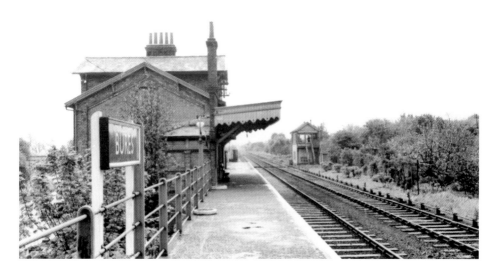

A general view looking south at Bures, taken in 1962, showing the original CSVS&H Railway building, canopy, goods loop and signal box. Freight traffic at Bures ceased to be handled on and from 28 December 1964. The signal box and goods loop were scheduled to be closed on 25 February 1965, but this was postponed until 6 September 1965. (Stations UK) Today, the same view shows an empty platform and a modern sign. The old station railings and lamp post confirm the location. (Paul Lemon)

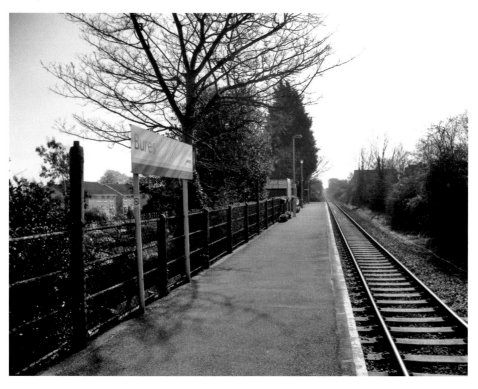

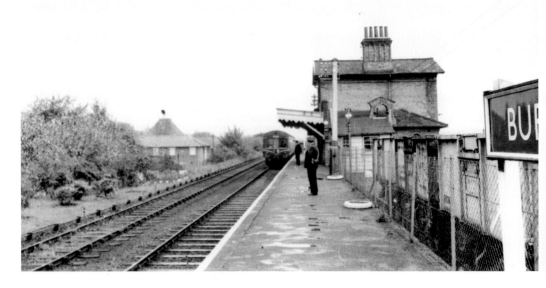

Up direction Diesel Multiple Unit arriving at Bures in 1962. The signalman is waiting on the platform to exchange tablets for the next single line section to Chappel & Wakes Colne. The loop line on the left could only be used to pass goods trains. (Stations UK)

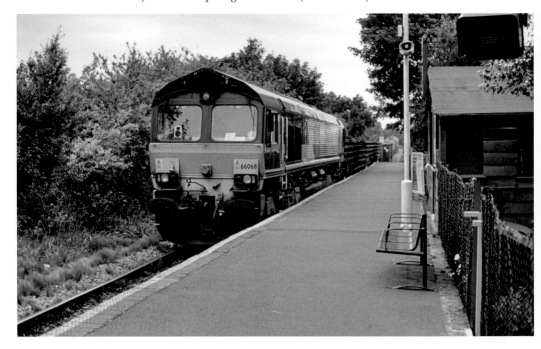

In 2005, when the engineers were relaying the branch track, we see diesel locomotive 66068 passing Bures platform proceeding back towards the main line at Marks Tey. The wooden waiting shelter can be seen on the right; the Maltings seen in the top picture are hidden behind the trees. (Ray Bishop)

Sudbury

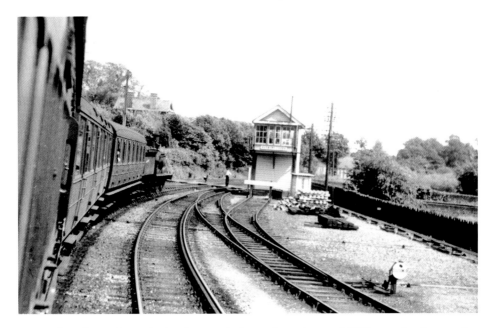

View taken from the train in the up platform, featuring ex-LNER type J15 locomotive 65390 looking towards Sudbury Goods Junction signal box, 7 July 1956. Note how clean and tidy the station was in those days. The wooden fence seen in the top picture still exists behind the trees on the lower view. (R. M. Casserley) Today, the station has been demolished, and a new platform on the site of the old loading dock has left all the other ground available for car parking – from which this view was taken looking towards the old signal box. (Paul Lemon)

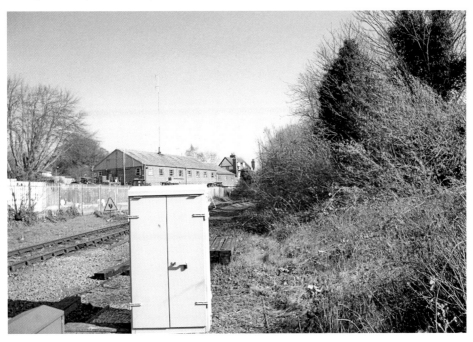

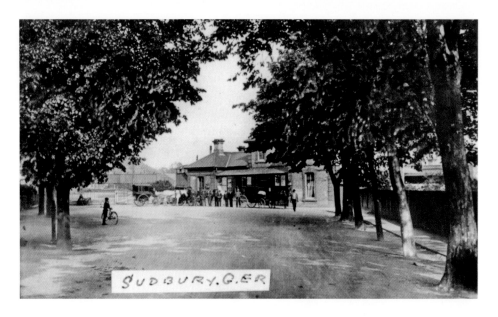

An old Great Eastern railway view of Sudbury station, taken from the tree-lined approach road in the early years of the twentieth century. The station was manned right up to 15 August 1966, and then spent some time as a small railway museum, before spending a number of years being boarded up. It was eventually demolished, to make way for a new car park and taxi rank. (Lens of Sutton Association) Today, there have been many alterations at Sudbury, but the tree-lined avenue seems to have survived all these changes. (Paul Lemon)

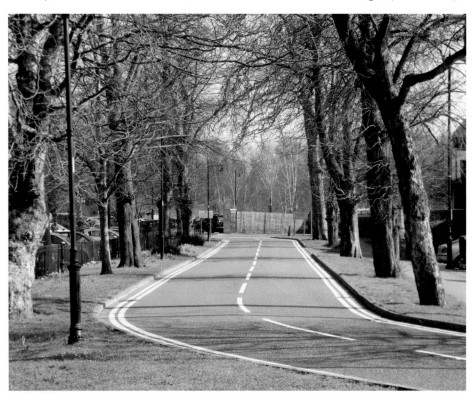

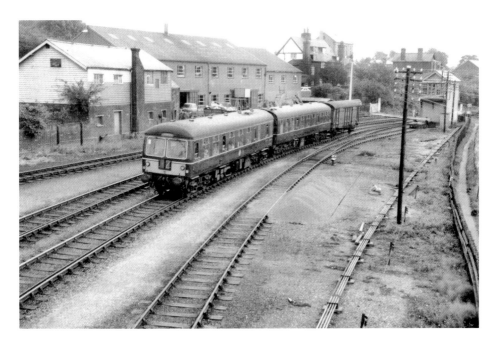

A two-car Diesel Multiple Unit with a tail van arriving at Sudbury station in the early 1960s, before any major reduction in facilities had taken place. This view was taken from a public footpath footbridge that spanned the layout at that time. (Dr I. C. Allen/Transport Treasury) Nearly twenty years later, the same view was taken as a two-car DMU entered the much-reduced station. All the goods sidings and platform lines have long since been removed. The signal box was still in use at this time, to control the adjacent level crossing and its two protecting signals. This anomaly was rectified in 1981, when the box was closed and demolished. (Andy T. Wallis)

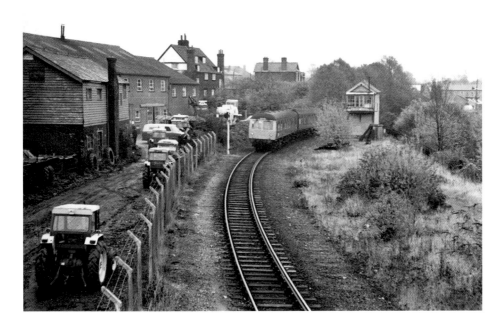

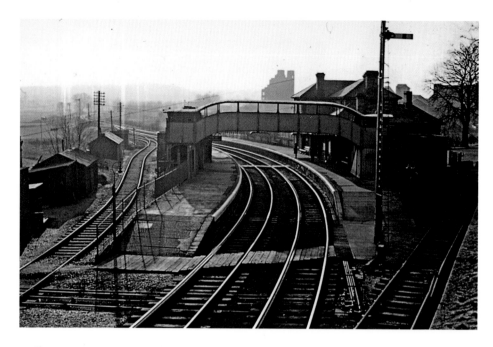

Sudbury station on a quiet Sunday morning, 5 March 1967, the day after trains had ceased to run beyond this point. The station and track layout is fully intact, free from weeds and litter. (Brian Pask) Some thirteen years later, it is a completely different story. All the track sidings have been lifted, leaving just the buffer stop at the end of the platform; the tall concrete starting signal has also been replaced nearer to the signal box. All the platform buildings on the down side have been demolished. The footbridge was to be eventually dismantled and moved to the Stour Valley Railway Museum at Chappel & Wakes Colne station. (Andy T. Wallis)

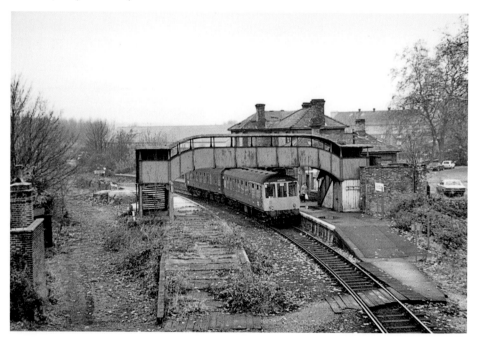

Sudbury Old CSVS&H Railway Station

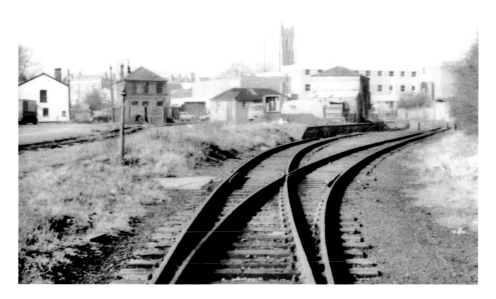

The old original Sudbury station as built for the Colchester, Stour Valley, Sudbury and Halstead Railway in 1849. This station was given over to goods traffic when the line was extended to Long Melford, Haverhill and Bury St Edmunds. Goods traffic continued to be handled at this station until it closed in 1966. The goods yard covered an extensive area next to the station, there being a number of sidings and wagon turntables leading to Maltings and an iron foundry. Several of the sidings crossed over Great Eastern Street to serve various industrial premises. (D. J. Plyer) Today, the whole of the former goods yard is now a supermarket and large car park. The common landmark is St Peter's church and the former Great Eastern Hotel is now a nightclub. (Paul Lemon)

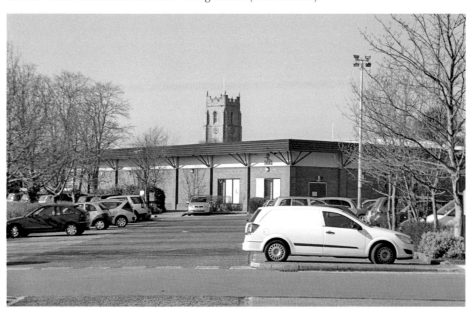

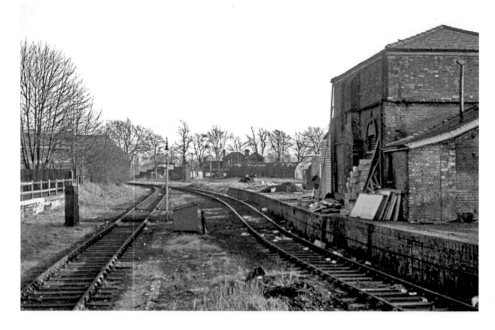

Another view of Sudbury goods station, looking from Great Eastern Street back towards the station. There were a number of old railway buildings to the right of this view that have all been demolished. (D. J. Plyer) Today, standing on the far side of Great Eastern Street, we see the edge of the supermarket, which marks the boundary of the former railway land. To the right and behind the supermarket is now all car park. (Paul Lemon)

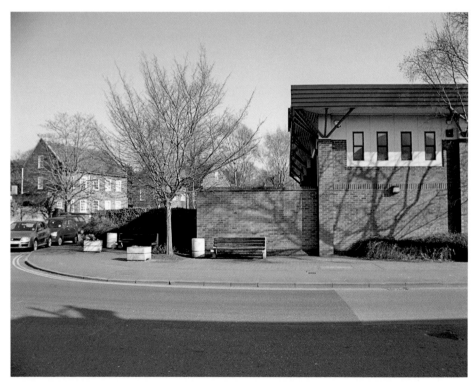

Long Melford

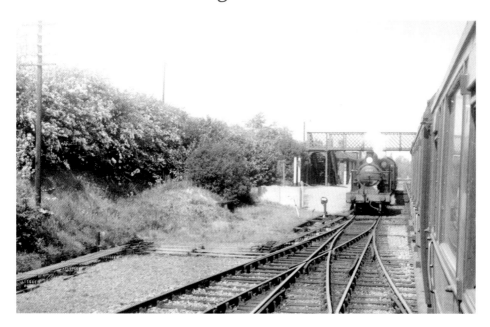

View taken from a train at Long Melford down platform, with a local train standing waiting to shunt, featuring ex-Great Northern locomotive, 67397, later classified as class C12 by the LNER. This picture was dated 26 May 1956, some three years before diesels were introduced on all local passenger services. (R. M. Casserley) The exact view cannot be reproduced now, as there are houses built on the end of the station platform. However, with the permission of the station owner, a similar view is shown with the old downside buildings and the edge of the former platform clearly visible. The space between the platforms has been filled in and grassed over. (Ray Bishop)

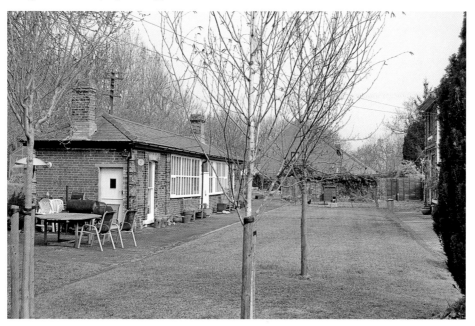

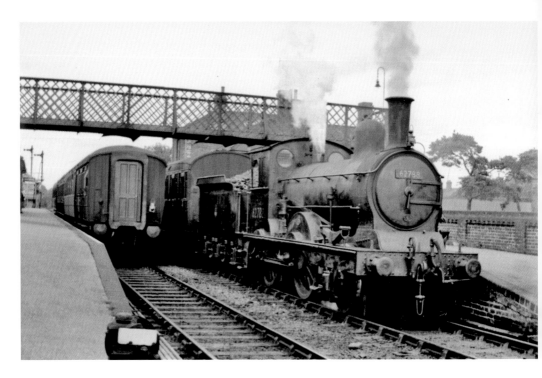

An ex-GER locomotive, later LNER class E4 number 62788, on an up passenger working, making connection with a down passenger working at Long Melford, 8 August 1956. Most Bury branch trains terminated at Long Melford, and the locomotive ran round its train ready for its next service. (Brian Pask) Today, the old station buildings have been made into a fine home. The grassed area is where the track was and the footbridge was demolished by BR before the line closed in 1967. (Ray Bishop)

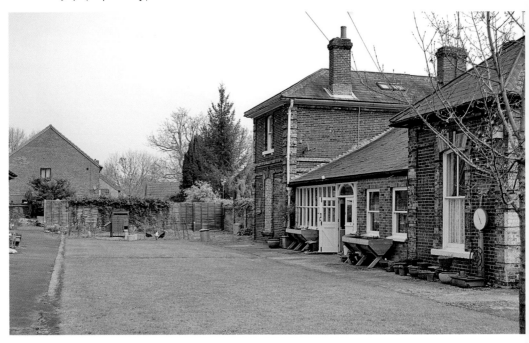

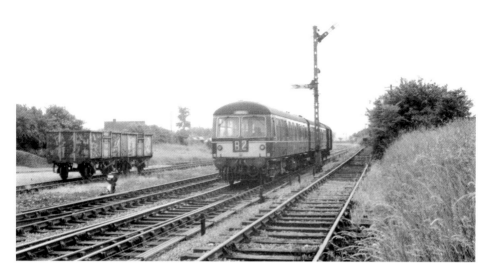

Local Diesel Multiple Unit plus tail traffic, arriving at Long Melford with a down direction service from Colchester and Sudbury. The signal seen in this view is the down home, which is sharing the post with the Rodbridges level crossing distant signal. The siding on the right connected with the down line at the station. The two tracks on the left are sidings at the end of the goods yard. DMUs and Rail Buses took over all local passenger services on the Stour, Colne and Bury branches from 1 January 1959. (Dr I. C. Allen/Transport Treasury) Today, the track has all gone and a housing development has been built on the former track bed and goods yard, although south of the houses the old formation can be reacquired, leading to the large river bridge over the River Stour near to Rodbridge level crossing. This view is of the former rail bridge as seen in 2011. (Ray Bishop)

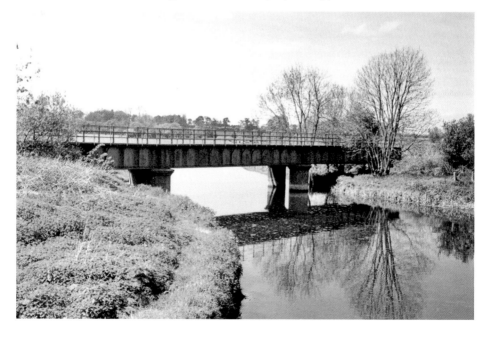

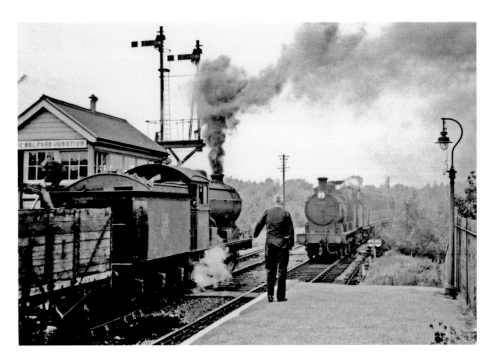

A busy scene on 16 August 1957, with ex-LNER J19 0-6-0 freight locomotive 64659 on a down freight service waiting for the road, and ex-LNER class J17 No. 65562 arriving on an up service at Long Melford Junction. The signalman is seen waiting to take the single line tablet from the arriving service. (Brian Pask) The end of the platforms and signal box site were sold off for housing, so in the view below, the third house in the distance is roughly where the previous view was taken. The area between the two platforms has been filled in, and makes a fine lawn, shared with chickens and a swimming pool – not in view. (Ray Bishop)

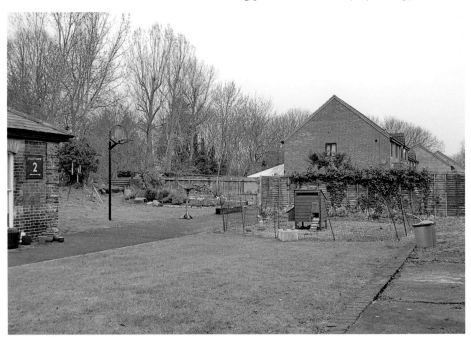

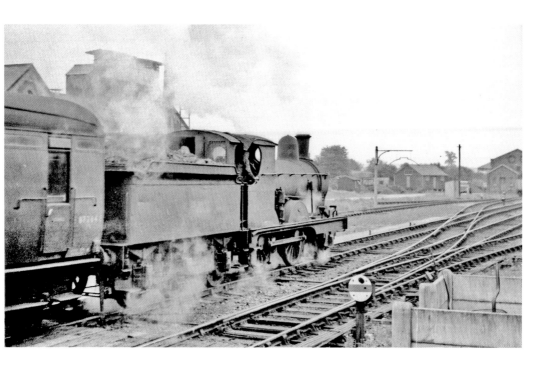

On the same day, at the other end of the station, an LNER class E4 departs towards Sudbury and Colchester with a local passenger working. The extensive goods yard is to the left of the locomotive. A down refuge siding was also situated opposite the goods yard. (Brian Pask) The far end of the platform has now been lost under the new houses, which overlook the former station site, although some screening has been provided by trees. The edge of the platform can be seen next to the garden chairs on the right of the picture. (Ray Bishop)

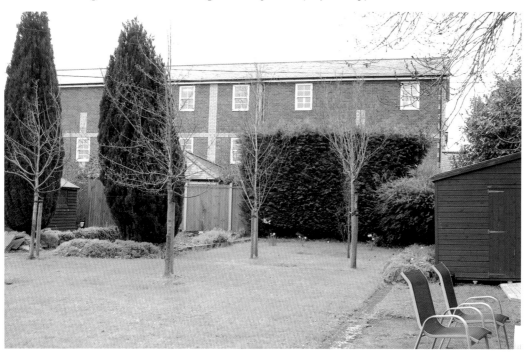

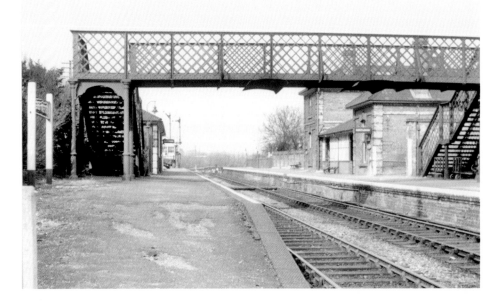

General view of Long Melford station looking northwards with the down starting signal off for the next Cambridge direction service. Long Melford station was equipped with the standard 1865 Great Eastern-type buildings on the up platform, with a large covered waiting room on the down platform. The platforms were connected by a footbridge. The signal box known as Long Melford Junction was originally fitted with a thirty-five-lever frame (later extended to forty-five levers), and had controlled all the layout since the Yard box closed in the 1930s. (R. M. Casserley) Long Melford as seen in 1979/80, with the main buildings then being used as offices for a local coach firm. Since then, all the former railway land to the north and south of the station site has been given over to housing development. (Andy T. Wallis)

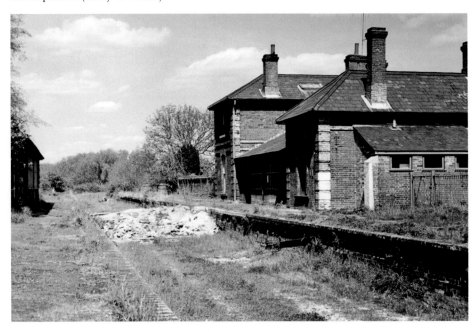

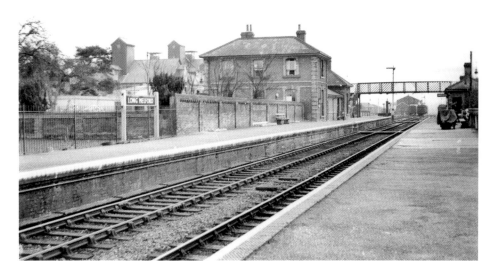

General view of Long Melford, looking south, with the main station's building on the up platform. Behind the Station Master's house can be seen the large Maltings that provided much traffic to the railway. At the end of the platform was the footbridge for crossing over to the down platform. This picture was taken on 6 April 1955. (R. M. Casserley) Twelve short years later, just two months from total closure of the line, we have a view taken from the down DMU service standing in the platform. The up service has just left the station en route to Sudbury and Colchester. Note that the station footbridge had been demolished by this time, as had the large goods shed seen in the distance in the top picture. Today's view would be of a private garden, with houses built on all the railway land to the south of the station. (Brian Pask)

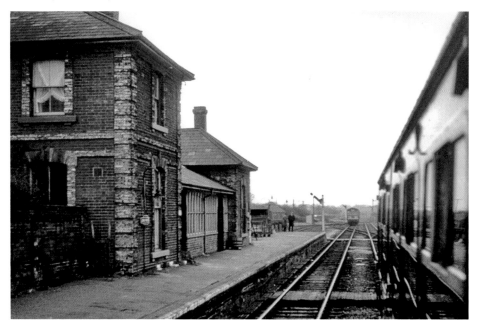

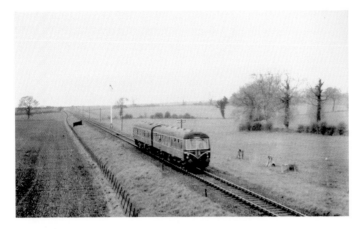

After departing from Long Melford, the Bury branch turned to the north-east for the journey to Lavenham. The next views were taken on the last day of regular passenger services over the branch, and feature two views of DMUs approaching Lavenham from the north and south. One picture features an old Great Eastern lower quadrant signal, and the other a more modern tubular steel upper quadrant with what would have been a BR replacement. (Brian Pask)

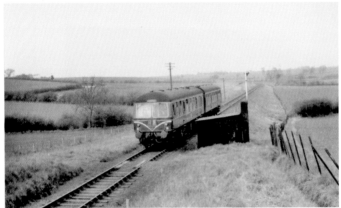

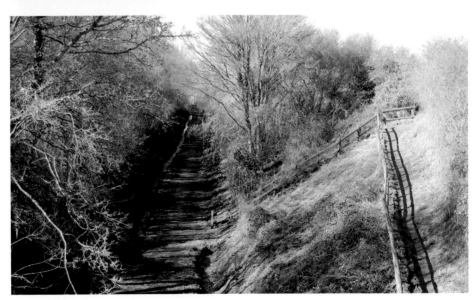

Today, nearly fifty years have passed, and it is pleasing to find part of the track bed on the southern approaches to Lavenham has been made into a public walkway called the 'Lavenham Walk', which ends at the former station site. (Ray Bishop)

Lavenham

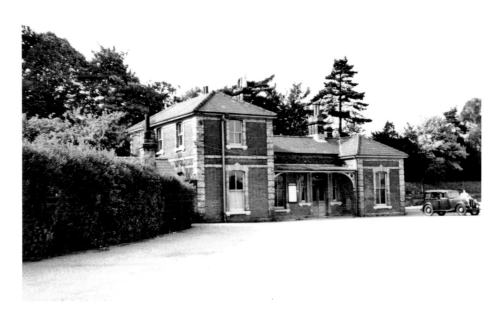

Lavenham station, taken from the forecourt, on a lovely summer's day in June 1965. Unfortunately, the last goods train had run from here in April 1965 and the old Great Eastern station was awaiting its fate. The station building and house was to survive for a number of years, whilst the goods yard was completely redeveloped into an industrial site. Many years later, the station building was demolished in favour of a large factory unit. (R. M. Casserley) The view in 2011 shows the replacement building occupying the station site. (Ray Bishop)

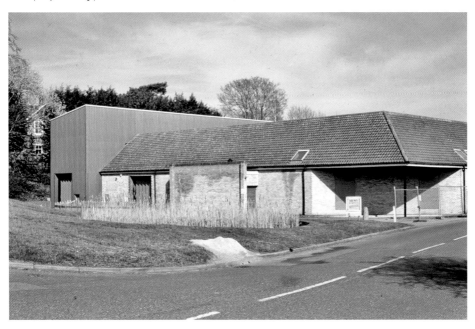

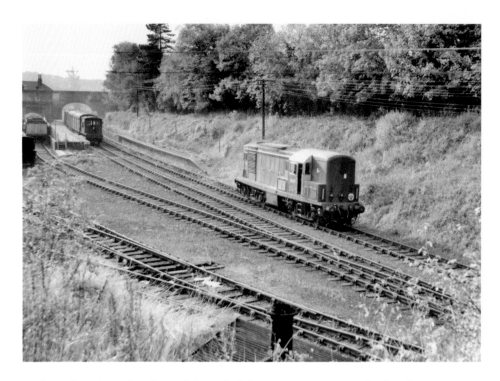

In the early 1960s, after the withdrawal of the passenger service, the freight service was provided from Bury St Edmunds, and we see Type 1 diesel D8227 running round its train at Lavenham. The view is looking towards Long Melford. In 1962, the track was lifted between Lavenham and Long Melford. (Dr I. C. Allen/Transport Treasury) Today, the railway has been completely obliterated at this location, with a large factory now occupying the former running lines and goods yard. (Ray Bishop)

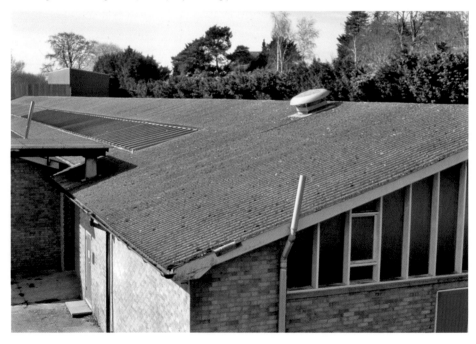

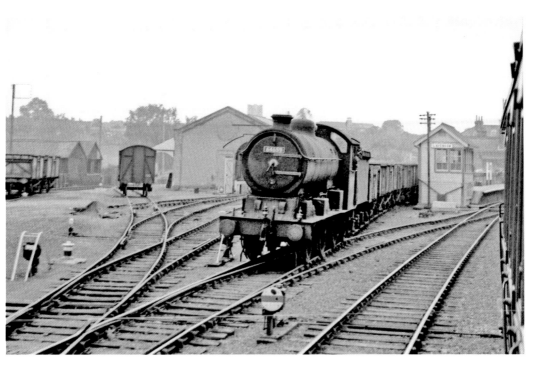

Ex-LNER large freight locomotive class J19 shunting mineral wagons at Lavenham. This view was taken from the down passenger train standing in the loop, waiting to pass an up service to Long Melford on 16 August 1957. The goods yard looked to be fairly busy at this time. (Brian Pask)

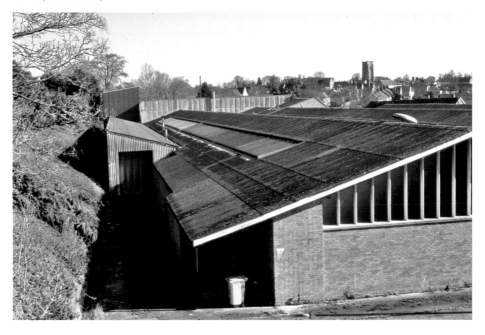

A similar view to the last picture, showing the large factory unit on the former railway land. The church tower in the distance is the common landmark. (Ray Bishop)

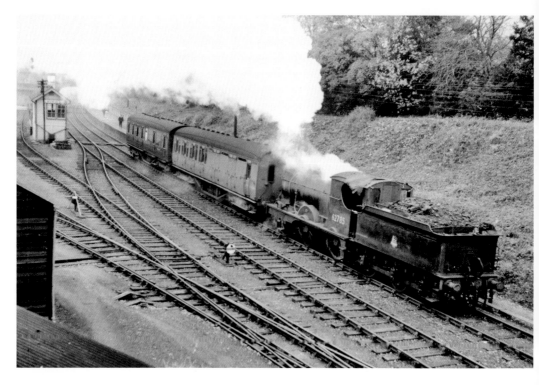

Ex-LNER class E4 and its two-coach train departs from Lavenham during the 1950s. From January 1959, DMUs replaced steam on the Bury St Edmunds to Long Melford local passenger services. (Dr I. C. Allen/Transport Treasury) Today, the view is again of the former station site. The bank on the right was the edge of the cutting and former platform. (Ray Bishop)

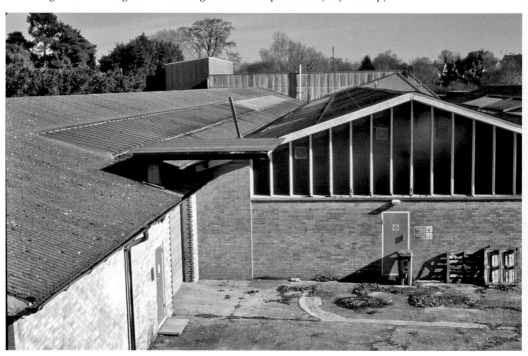

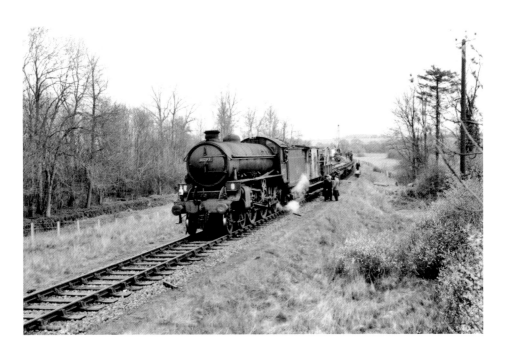

After the withdrawal of the local passenger service in April 1961, there was one other passenger service that was to travel over the whole of the branch; this was a diesel-hauled Ramblers' Special, which ran in June 1961. After that, the line between Lavenham and Long Melford was closed, and track-lifting took place in early 1962. This view is of a demolition train, working from the Lavenham end, lifting the track. (Dr I. C. Allen/Transport Treasury) Today, two portions of the old railway track bed exist between Long Melford and Lavenham, the first is at the Long Melford end, known as the Melford Walk, whilst the second, shown here, is the Lavenham Walk. (Ray Bishop)

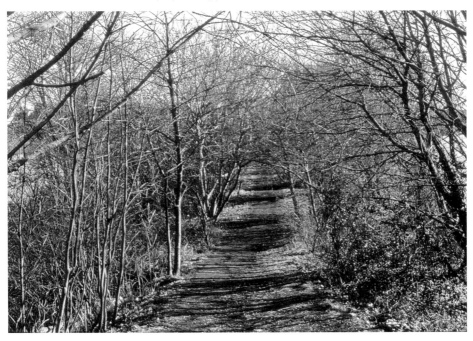

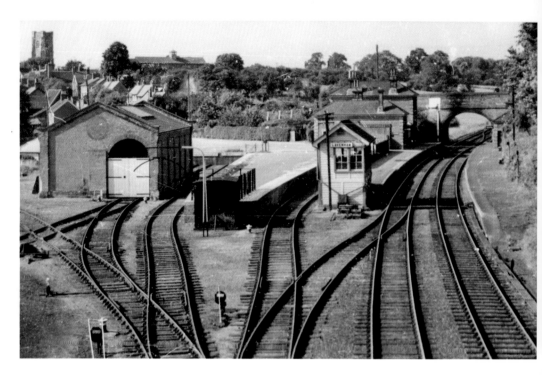

A general view of Lavenham station, taken from the road bridge at the northern end of the station, showing the large goods shed, signal box and station buildings. Lavenham church can be seen on the far left in the background. (Rail Archive Stephenson) After the complete closure of the railway at Lavenham, the former goods yard was sold off for industrial development (*see previous pictures*). As an alternative to more views of factories, the view below, taken in the 1950s, shows a busy goods yard and a neat and tidy station waiting for its next passengers. (Stations UK)

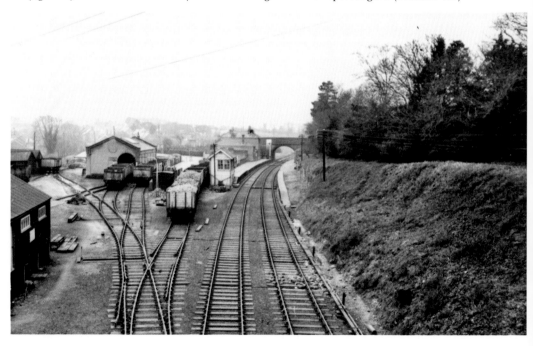

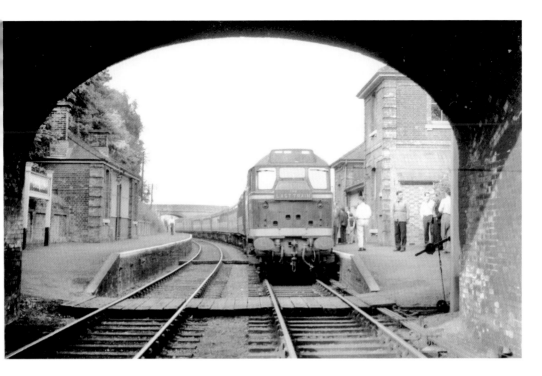

Brush Type 2 diesel locomotive No. D5537 (later Class 31), on the return Ramblers' Special, standing at Lavenham waiting departure to the south. This was the last train to travel over the complete branch. It had originated earlier in the day at London Liverpool Street and had traversed the whole branch in both directions. (Brian Pask) Today, the rail bridge marks the end of the Lavenham Walk. Beyond this point, all of the former railway infrastructure has been swept away and new factory units occupy the site. (Ray Bishop)

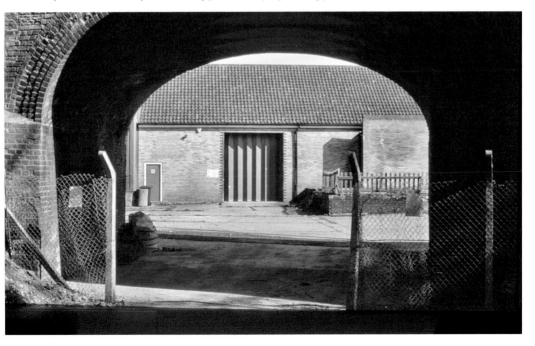

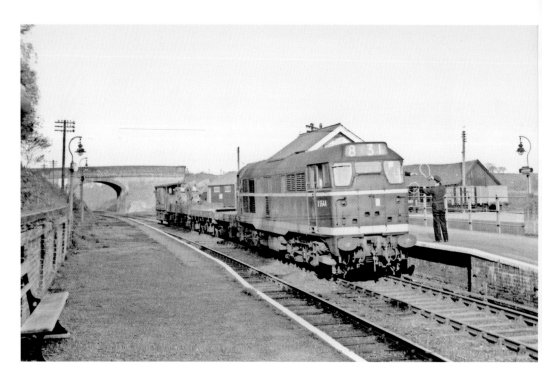

The signalman exchanges tokens with the driver of the last through freight over the branch on 8 April 1961. Following withdrawal of the passenger service, Lavenham became the end of the line for freight traffic running to and from Bury St Edmunds. The line south of Lavenham was dismantled in early 1962, part of which is now the 'Lavenham Walk'. (Brian P. Pask)

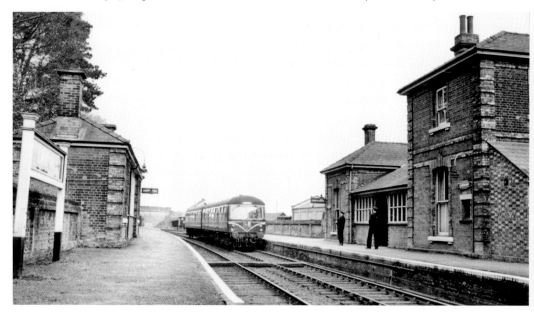

The passenger services over the line were operated by DMUs from 1 January 1959, and in this view a southbound diesel unit is calling en route to Long Melford. The use of diesels was short-lived, as the passenger service was withdrawn in April 1961. (Stations UK)

Cockfield

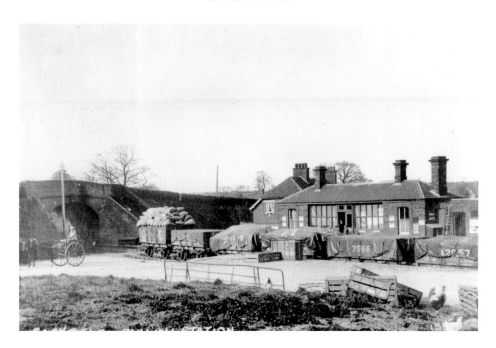

Cockfield station in the Great Eastern days, with a rake of fully loaded wagons waiting to depart on the next goods service. Note the pony and trap on the left of the view. The single-storey Cockfield station building was located at the Bury St Edmunds end of the single platform. (Lens of Sutton Association) Today, the station buildings still stand, although in need of some maintenance work. The track bed has been grassed over but is kept in good order. (Ray Bishop)

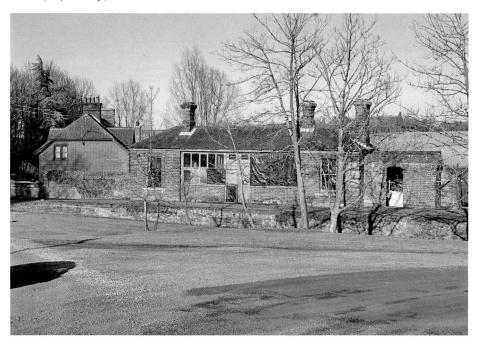

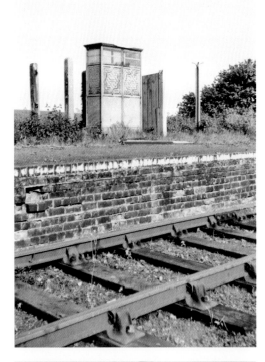

The cast-iron gents' urinal 'building' at Cockfield station, 5 June 1965, after the station had closed completely but prior to the track being lifted. (R. M. Casserley)

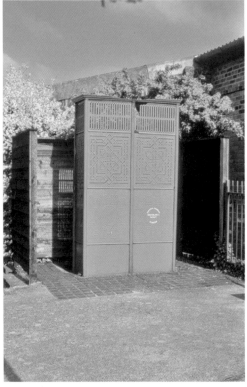

The cast-iron gents' urinal was salvaged and found its way to the East Anglia Railway Museum at Chappel & Wakes Colne for display as a genuine Great Eastern artefact. (Ray Bishop)

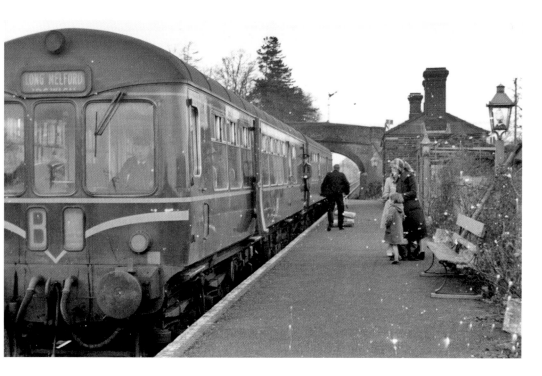

Wickham's type Diesel Multiple Unit calls at Cockfield en route to Long Melford, on a cold winter's day, 1960/61. There seem to be only three passengers, one alighting and two boarding. Loadings of this nature led to the early withdrawal of the passenger service in April 1961. (David Lawrence)

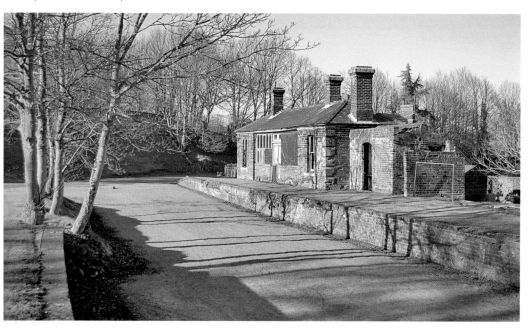

A view taken from the former loading dock, showing the main station building and platform. The road bridge has been filled in and planted with trees. (Ray Bishop)

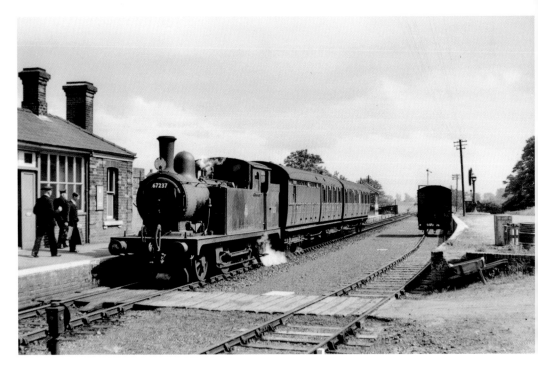

An elderly 2-4-2 tank engine designated LNER class F6 number 67237 arrives at Cockfield station with a down passenger service for Bury St. Edmunds. The date of this view is not known, but looks to mid-1950s. (Dr I. C. Allen/Transport Treasury) The close-up of the station and platform shown below, taken from a similar view, shows the poor state of the building and platform edge. The owner who allowed access for these pictures sells bagged coal from the other end of the station. (Ray Bishop)

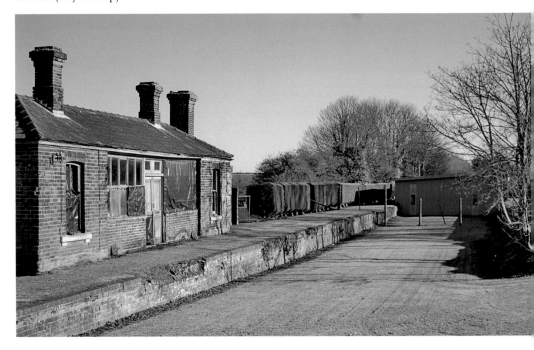

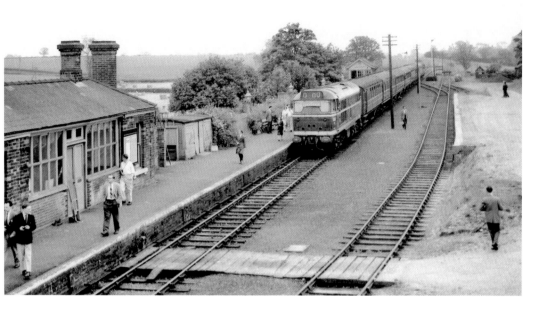

Brush Type 2 diesel locomotive No. D5537 arrives at Cockfield with the last through train over the complete branch. This was a Ramblers' Special that had originated at London Liverpool Street earlier in the day, 4 June 1961. Cockfield station would remain open to handle freight traffic until April 1965. (Brian Pask) Below, a further image taken from the road bridge creates a similar view to the top picture. Trains last ran through this station in April 1965, some forty-five years ago. (Ray Bishop)

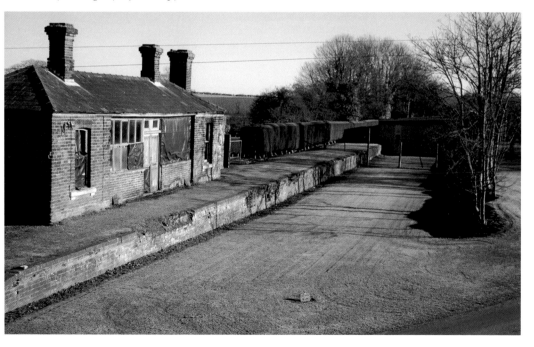

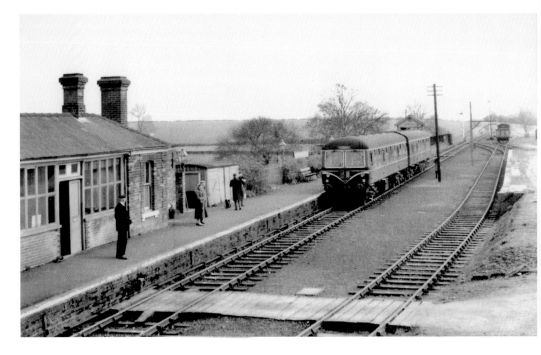

A similar view to the previous, but this time taken on the last day of passenger workings with a down DMU on a local working to Bury St Edmunds. There look to be four passengers and one member of staff. (Brian P. Pask)

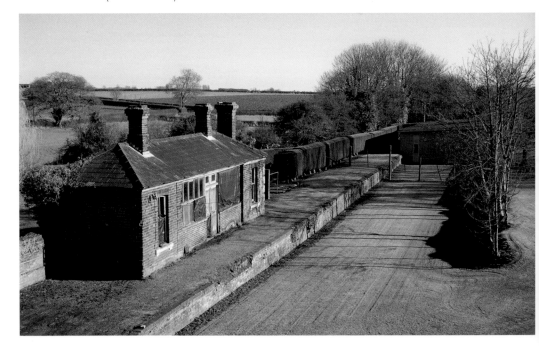

Another view from the former road over the rail bridge, looking south towards Long Melford. Access to the former station houses is by a track below the bridge, which continues down to the former goods yard. (Ray Bishop)

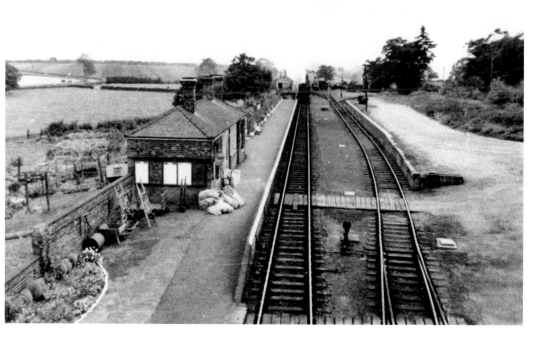

A general view, taken in 1953, from the road over the bridge; looking south, with the single-storey station building on the left and the goods loop/siding on the right. The signal box was at the far end of the platform and was equipped with an eighteen-lever Dutton frame. (Stations UK) The panoramic view below shows the station, platform and signal box, taken in 1953. (Stations UK)

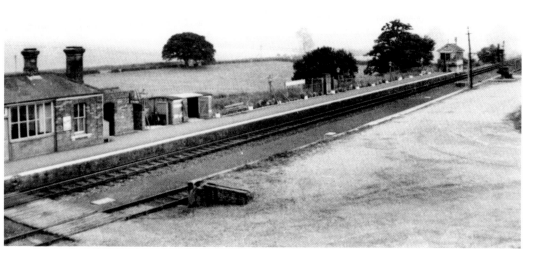

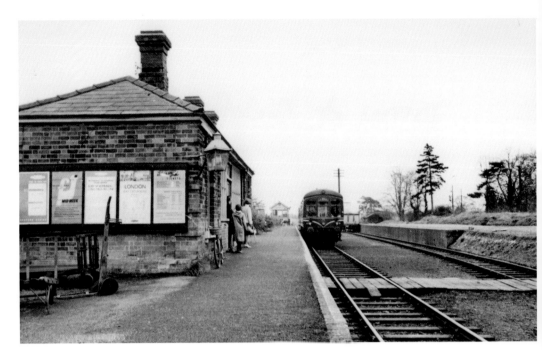

DMU comparisons: by 1961, the passenger service on the branch was condemned, due to be stopped in April of that year. A Derby Lightweight type DMU is seen arriving at Cockfield with a local working to Bury St Edmunds. Two or three passengers seemed to be waiting for the train. (Stations UK) Turning 180 degrees, we see a Cravens Diesel Multiple Unit arriving on a Long Melford service in the last few weeks of the passenger service. (Stations UK)

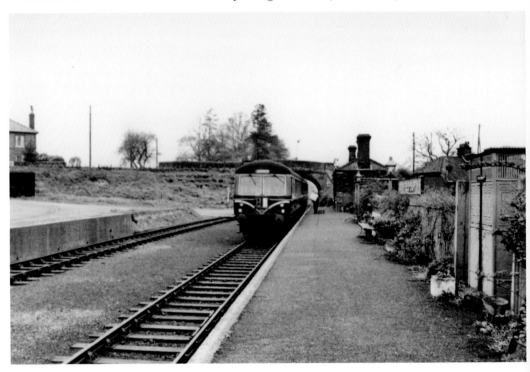

Welnetham

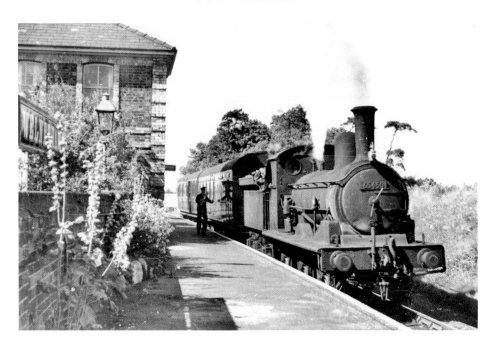

Ex-LNER class J15 No. 65450 arriving on a southbound local passenger service, in the 1950s, at Welnetham. There seem to be very few passengers, so the two-coach train would seem to be more than adequate. The Bury line benefited from the modernisation of stock, with DMUs and Rail Buses taking over all the passenger workings from 1 January 1959. (Rail Archive Stephenson) Today, the station survives as a private residence, and has been lovingly looked after during the forty-five years since it closed as a railway. The track bed now forms a pleasant, lawned area. The 1865 Great Eastern-style building is clearly seen. (Ray Bishop)

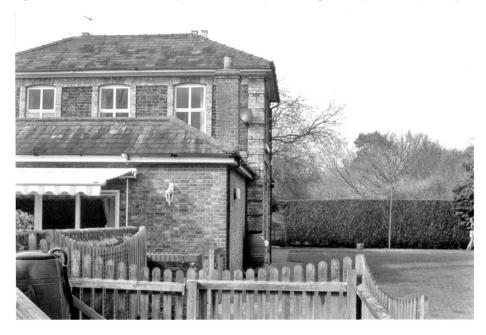

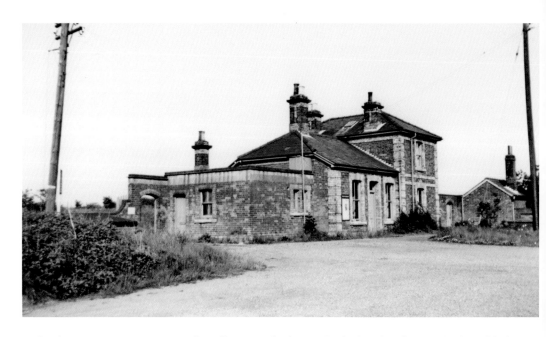

Welnetham station, 5 June 1965, after all services had ceased. The last freight train had rumbled north from here in April 1965. The rails were still down, awaiting the arrival of the scrap man or demolition train. (R. M. Casserley) The station is still standing and is now a private residence. The classic 1865 GER-type station buildings can clearly be seen. A fence to the front and side has now been erected. (Roy Williams)

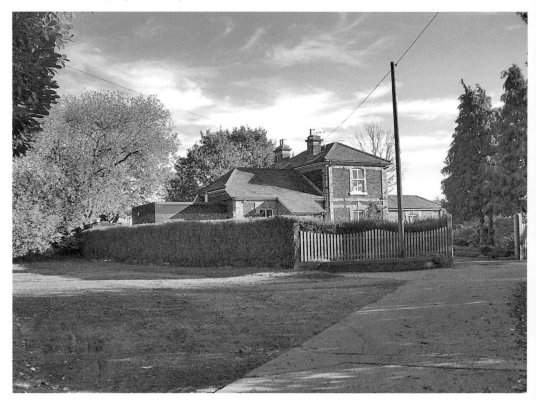

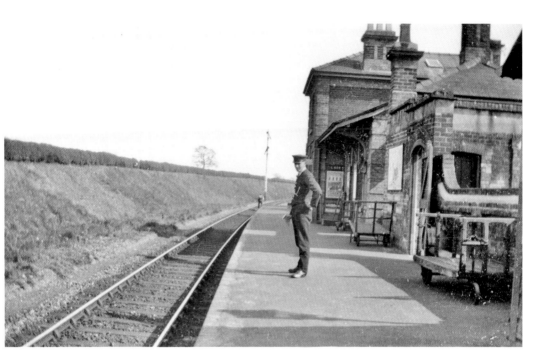

Two contrasting views: the first taken in the 1920s, with a porter standing on the platform. At this time, the station still had a signal box. As can be seen, everything was clean and tidy. (Stations UK) Forty years later, the scene has completely changed, with weeds growing up through the platform giving an uncared-for look to the place. The last train had run some two months before, and the track was awaiting the scrap man. Fortunately, the station survived and is now a private residence. (R. M. Casserley)

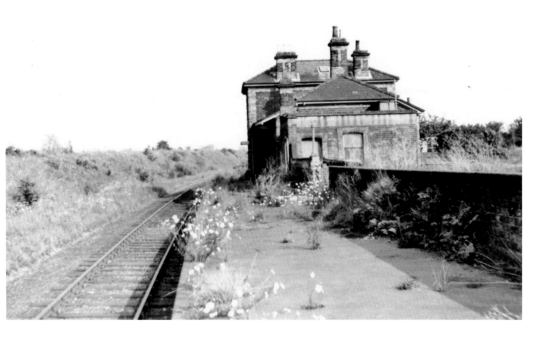

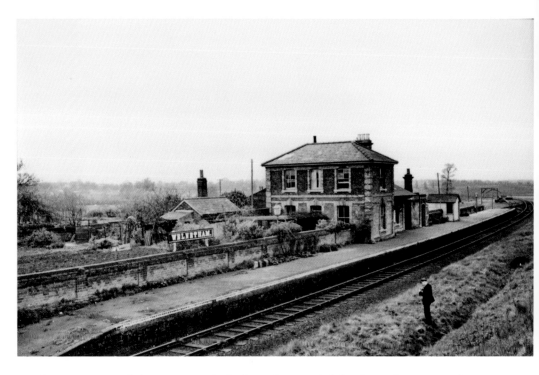

Another 1961 view, of the station and platform from a slightly elevated position. This view is looking north-west. The splendid station sign is now part of the national collection at the National Railway Museum, York. (Stations UK) Today, the station is a private house. With permission, this view was taken from what would have been the track bed, which has been filled in up to platform level. (Roy Williams)

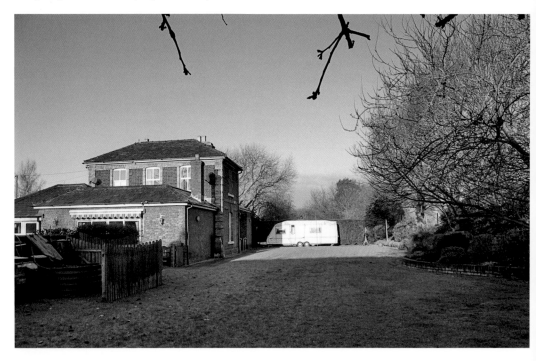

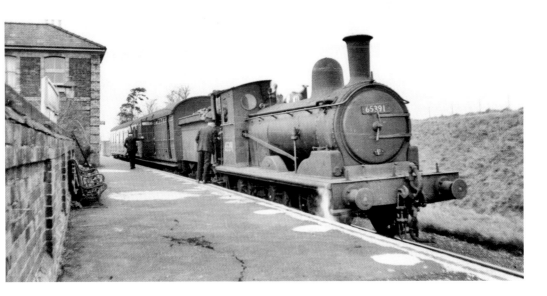

Locomotive 65391 awaits time during the 1950s, with its two-coach local passenger service. The branch benefited from the modernisation plan when diesels took over all the workings in 1959. (Stations UK)

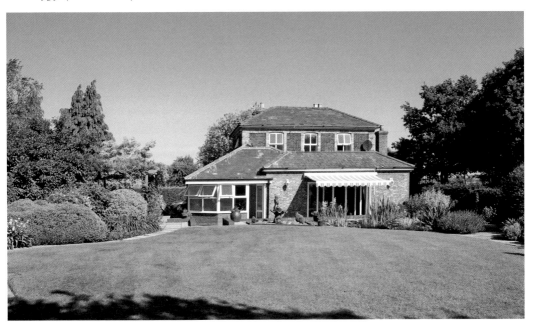

The former Station Master's garden and surrounding land has been turned into a fantastic garden. The classic lines of the 1865 GER-type buildings can clearly be seen. Trains would have run to the right of this picture. (Roy Williams)

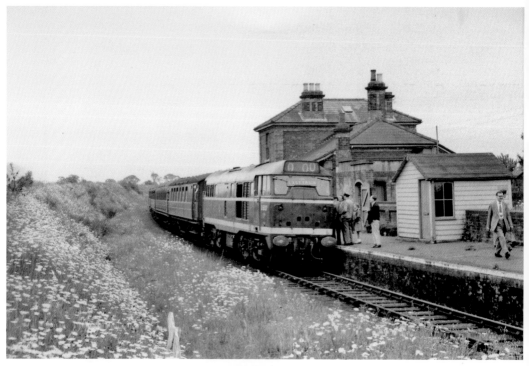

Above: Brush Type 2 (later class 31) pauses at Welnetham whilst working the Ramblers' Special in June 1961. This was the last through working over the whole line, the track between Lavenham and Long Melford was lifted during early 1962. (Brian Pask)

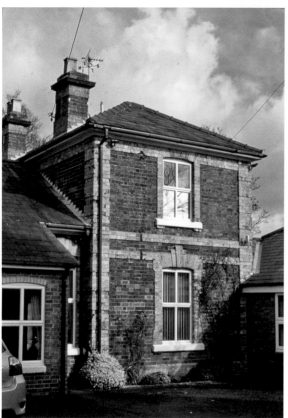

Left: Today, all is quiet as the track bed now forms part of the lawn in front of the main buildings. This view is of the original Station Master's house, now a fine private dwelling. (Ray Bishop)

Bury East Gates

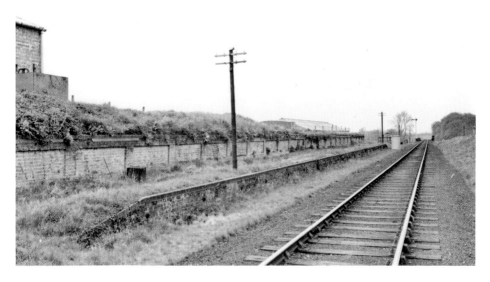

Some 30 miles and 30 chains from Marks Tey was Bury East Gates station. It opened for passenger traffic 9 August 1865. In 1889, the whole of the Stour Valley line was re-signalled to modern standards, with block working between Bury East Gates and Bury St Edmunds Junction being in force from 1890. The station at East Gates never fulfilled its passenger potential, and the station and signal box closed in June 1909. It did reopen for two days in June 1914 to serve the Suffolk Agricultural Show. The buildings were demolished leaving just a bare platform. This is the view looking north in 1961, showing the old platform. (Stations UK) The whole area is now factory units, with the A14 trunk road located behind the hedges. (Ray Bishop)

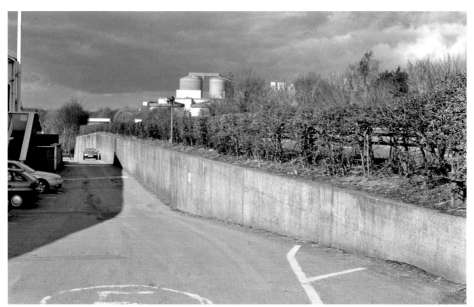

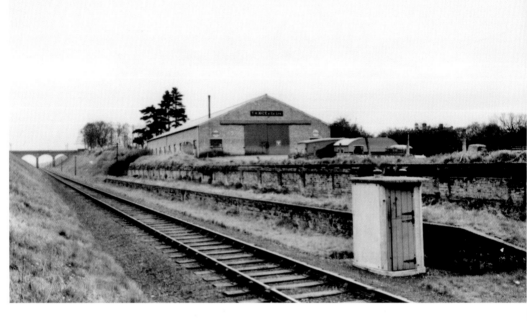

The former Bury East Gates station, looking south, with a nice three-arched bridge in the distance. This view was taken in 1961. (Stations UK) As in the previous picture, part of the former railway formation forms the A14 trunk road. This side of the hedges is an industrial park. (Ray Bishop)

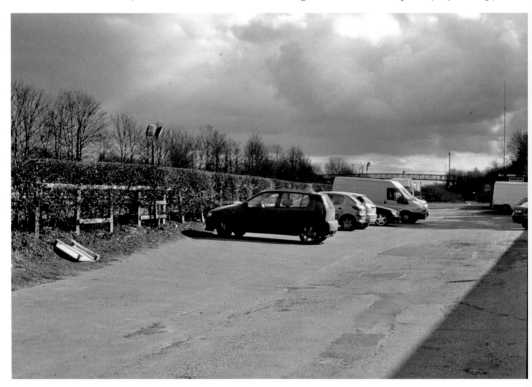

Bury St Edmunds

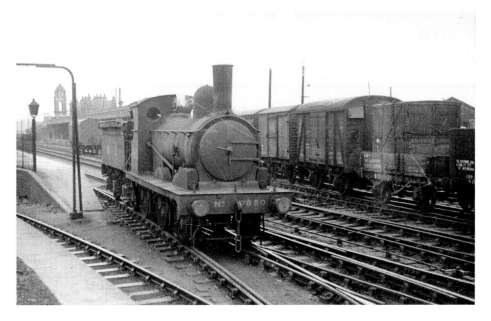

Locomotive number 7850, in LNER days, exits from a Bury St Edmunds shed to take up its next duty. A goods train waits on the down line. (H. C. Casserley) The similar view today looks from west to east towards Ipswich. By this time, the centre roads had long been lifted. The train service today is mostly made up of Diesel Multiple Units with cross country loco-hauled freight making up the rest of the traffic. (Ray Bishop)

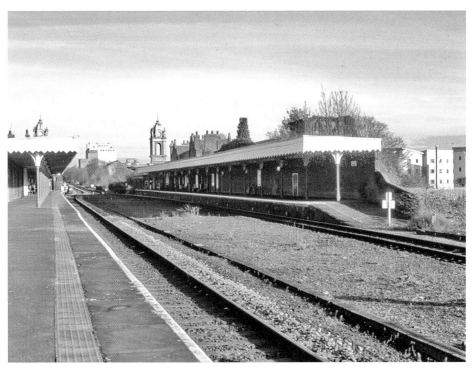

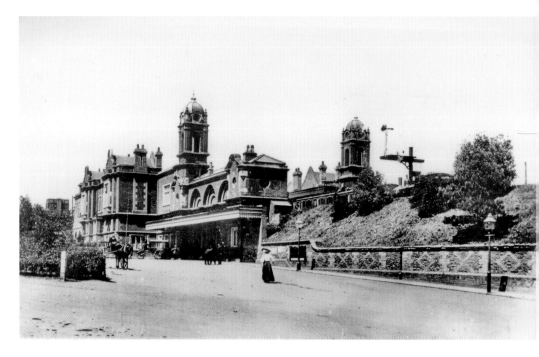

An old Great Eastern days view of the main buildings at Bury St Edmunds, with its splendid towers at the Ipswich end of the station. These buildings still stand today, despite the reduction in track and signalling at platform level. (Lens of Sutton Association) On a beautiful clear morning in February this year, we have the view today with all the main buildings intact. The trees on the right are obscuring the other tower. (Ray Bishop)

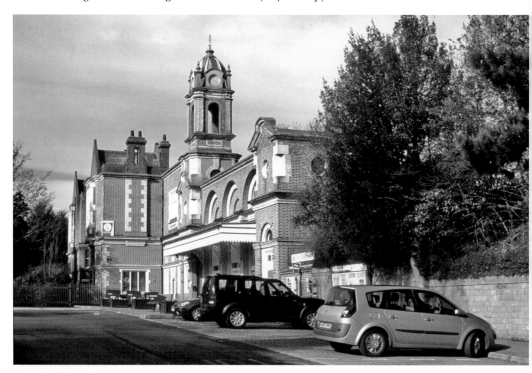

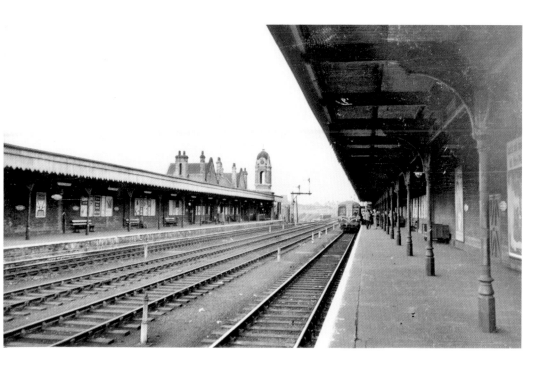

A general platform view looking east towards Ipswich with a local DMU service from Long Melford in the platform, seen in early 1961 prior to the withdrawal of the passenger service. Bury was provided with full-length excursion platforms and through-roads avoiding the platforms. (Stations UK) Today, the view is very similar except for the missing centre roads. It is pleasing to see the canopies still intact. (Ray Bishop)

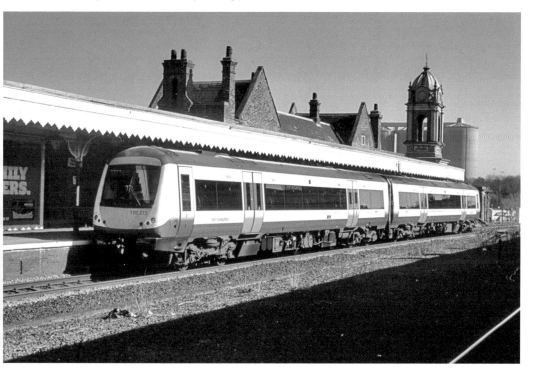

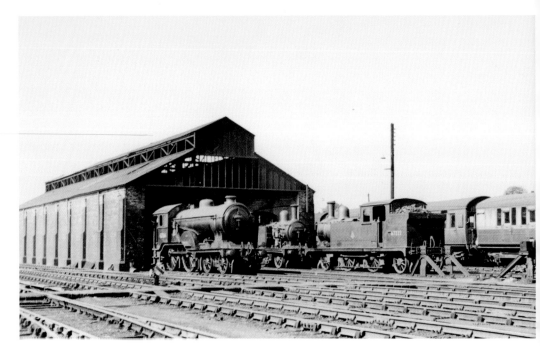

Locomotives 62566, 67236 and 67222 are spotted outside Bury St Edmunds locomotive depot and shed, 19 September 1953. The shed occupied a large site on the left as you approached the station from the Cambridge direction. After the closure of the locomotive shed, the area was used by the engineers to dismantle track components. (H. C. Casserley) There is nothing left of the former loco shed today, as a class 170 DMU arrives at the station passing Bury St Edmunds Yard signal box on the left. (Ray Bishop)

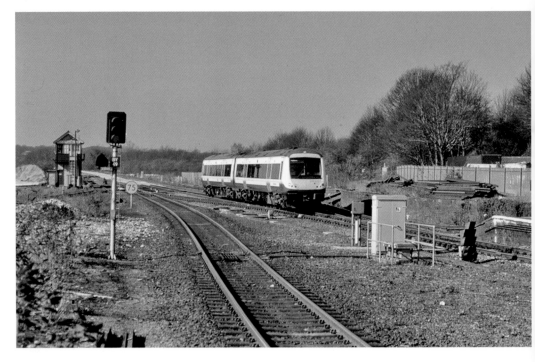

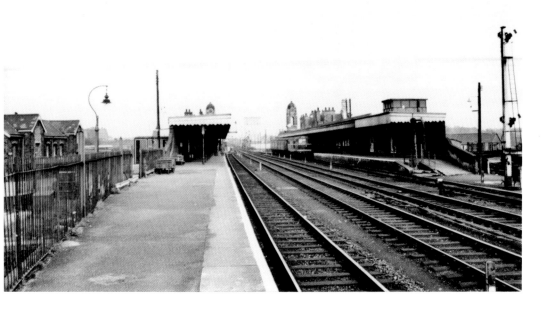

A 1961 view taken from the down platform, looking in an easterly direction, with a diesel-hauled passenger train in the up platform. The other lines, from left to right, were the down platform, down through and up through siding. (Stations UK) Today, the down through and up through siding tracks have been lifted. The rest of the station remains as seen in the top view. Loco-hauled passenger trains are now rarely seen on the line. (Ray Bishop)

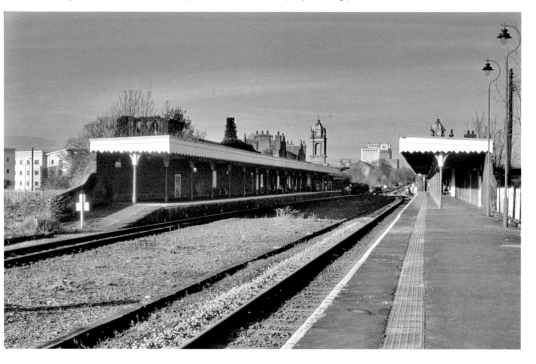

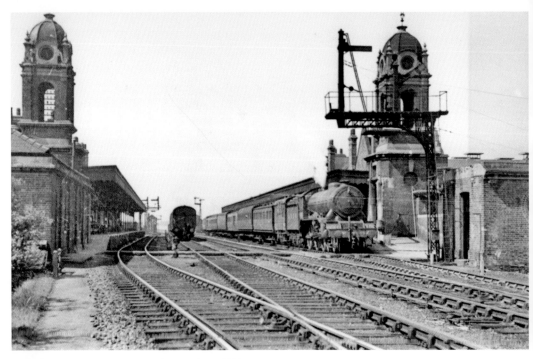

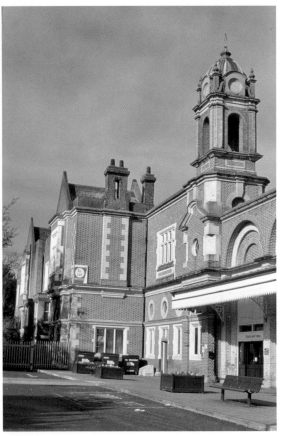

Above: A westerly view from the up cess, looking at the up platform on the left, with a train signalled away from the down platform on the right, 1948. This view shows a close-up of the two towers at the eastern end of the station. (Stations UK)

Left: A close-up of the towers, as seen from road level outside the station. (Ray Bishop)

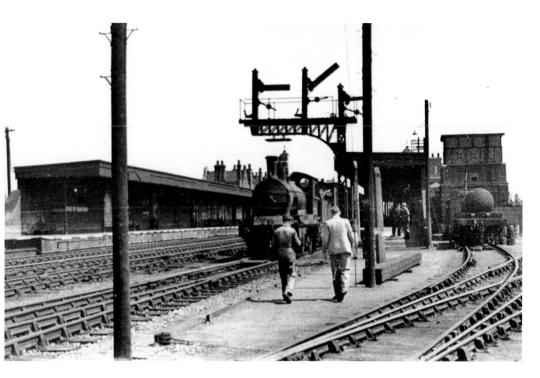

A general view taken from the upside yard of the station, with an up passenger train signalled to leave the station. This view was taken in 1948, just after nationalisation, although no changes were evident at this time. (Stations UK) The lower picture, also taken in 1948, features an overall view of the station, with plenty of traffic in the yard to the right – most of which is now conveyed by road. (Stations UK)

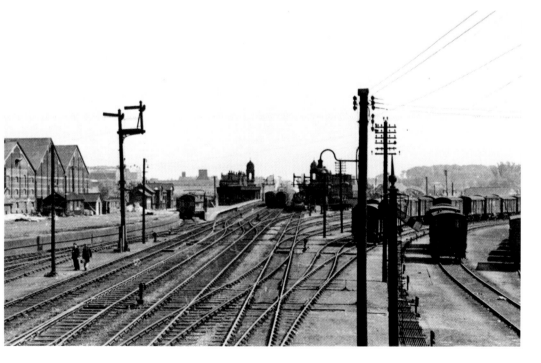

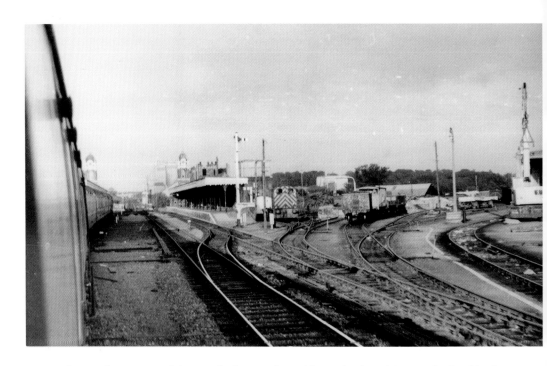

A view from a down train of the up platform and up side yard, taken 6 June 1965. By this time, the down through line had been removed and the down platform line was renamed the down main. The up through siding was now just a stabling siding reached from the Cambridge end of the layout only. (H. C. Casserley) As a contrast, the view below is of the road bridge – crossed by the railway – to get to the former Bury St Edmunds Junction, where our branch to the south commenced. Today, the first part of the branch is buried under the A14 Bury Bypass. (Ray Bishop)

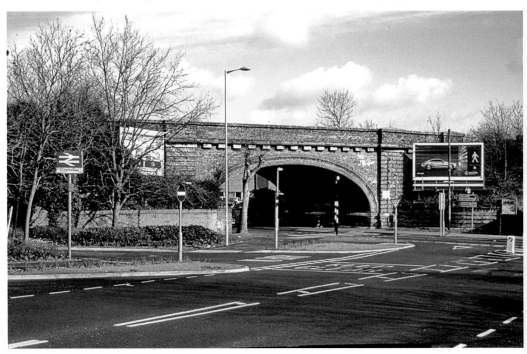

Long Melford Junction & Liston Level Crossing

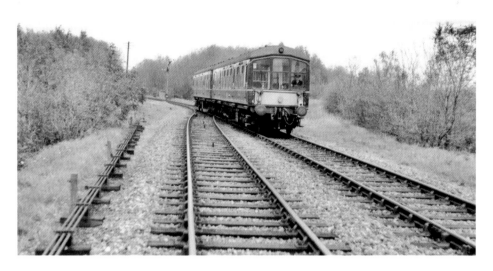

A Diesel Multiple Unit approaching the former Long Melford Junction in the early 1960s after the Bury branch had been lifted. The signal in the background is the up home signal for Long Melford, and the down gate distant for Liston level crossing. (Dr I. C. Allen/ Transport Treasury) The former Liston level crossing, now completely obliterated. The gatepost gives a clue to its previous use, as does the crossing keeper's house being an 1865 GE-designed structure. (Ray Bishop)

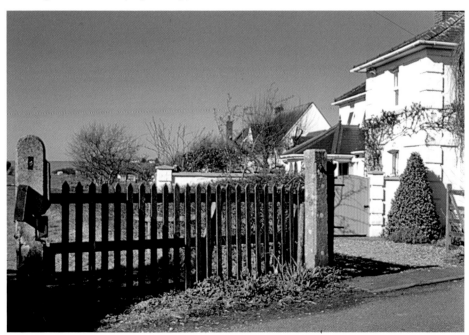

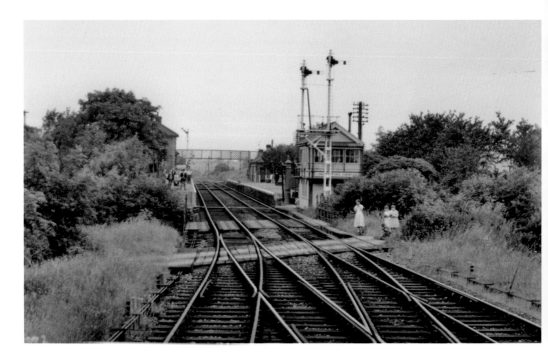

Long Melford Junction, as seen from the front cab of a DMU arriving at the station. The accommodation level crossing gave access to some houses behind the station, as did the bridge beyond it. There was very limited clearance on the bridge. (A. E. Bennett/Transport Treasury) Today, the railway is long gone, with only the brick abutments of the under-bridge giving a clue to the location. Some houses have been built between the bridge and the old station, on the site of the old signal box and part of the platforms. (Ray Bishop)

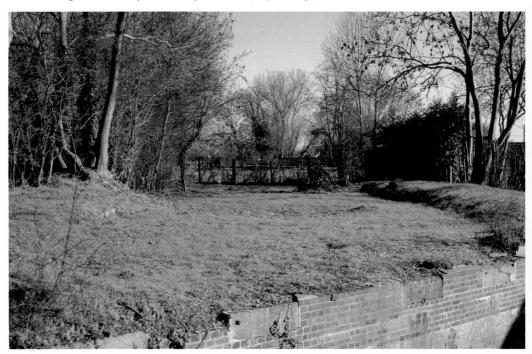

Glemsford

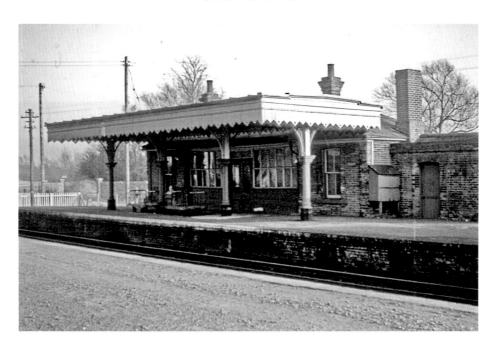

A rare colour view of Glemsford station building and canopy. When Glemsford station opened there was no canopy provided. This came later, courtesy of the GER. After closure, the platform buildings and canopy were demolished; however, the columns, brackets and main supporting timbers were kept and eventually sold to the new Colne Valley Railway for reuse. (Brian Pask)

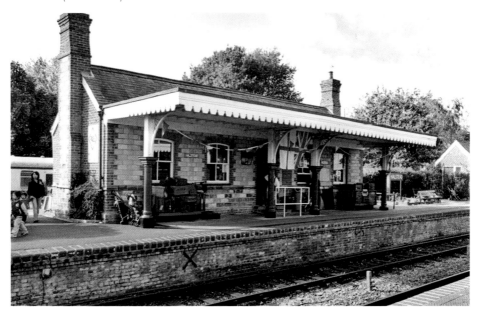

The canopy at Castle Hedingham down side building, featuring the columns, brackets and wooden timbers from Glemsford in good use at their second home. (Andy T. Wallis)

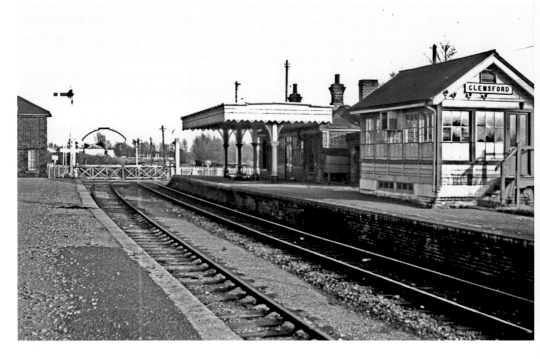

Another 1960s colour picture of Glemsford station buildings, canopy, signal box and level crossing gates. Note the loading gauge on the siding/loop line to the left of this view. (Brian Pask)

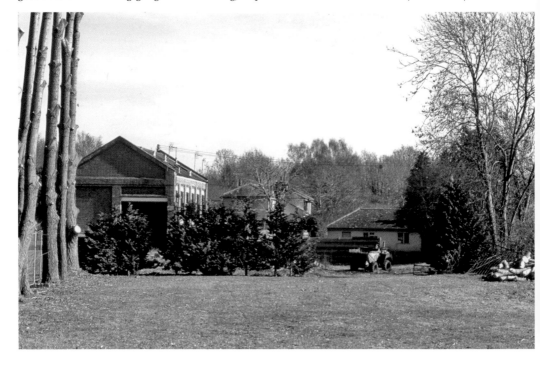

Today, the railway track and platforms have gone and the rest is used as a garden, with a garage and shed built at the level crossing end of the site. (Ray Bishop)

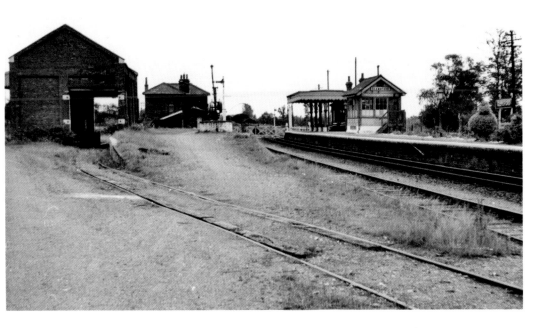

Comparisons: the black-and-white view of the station layout, taken in the late 1950s, shows the goods shed and station cottages on the left and the station buildings and platform on the right. There was a siding that runs from the loop line to serve the goods shed and loading platform. (CVRPS Ltd Collection) A similar view, this time in colour, shows all of the above items on 5 March 1967, the day after the last trains had run. Today, the goods shed has been converted into apartments. (Brian Pask)

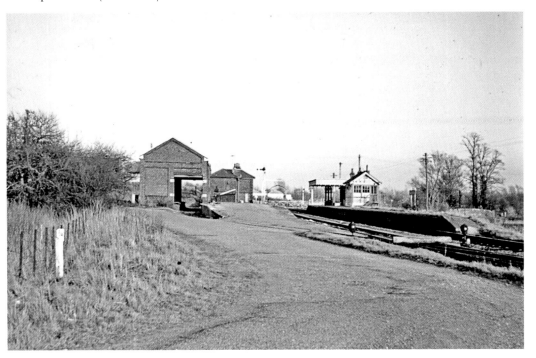

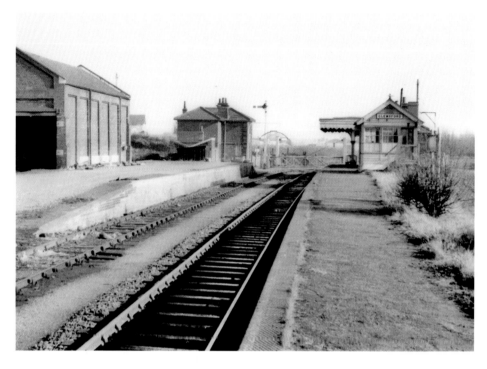

Glemsford station looking east, taken from the single platform. The platform on the left was used for loading wagons, the goods shed is built of brick with a slated roof and had a loading crane on the far side. This building has since been converted into living accommodation. (D. J. Plyer)

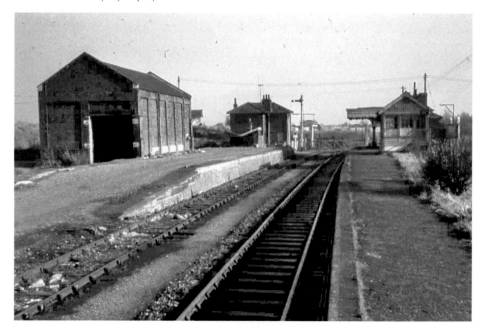

Below is the same view, 18 February 1967, a few weeks before the line closed completely. (D. J. Plyer)

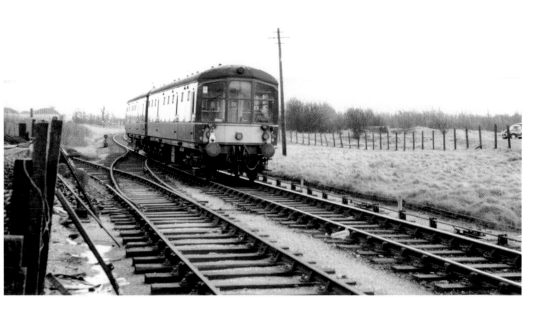

A two-car Derby Lightweight Diesel Multiple Unit departs from Glemsford towards Long Melford and Sudbury. On the left are the loop/siding points joining the main single line, with a short head shunt adjacent to the coal-stacking ground. (Dr I. C. Allen/Transport Treasury) Today, the view is gone and the coal-stacking ground is just a memory. Parts of the track bed at this location have been ploughed in or built over. (Ray Bishop)

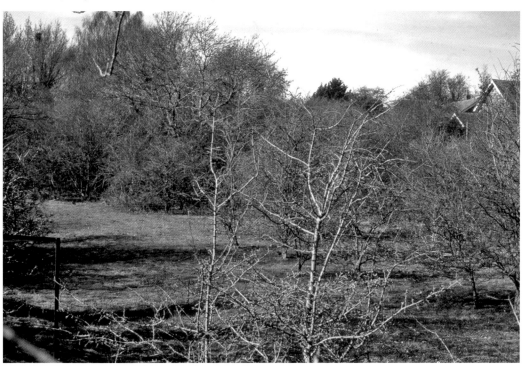

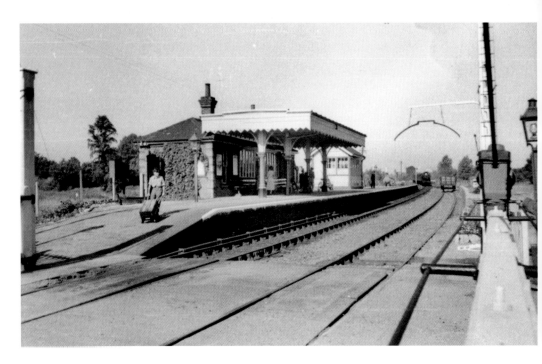

A view looking west, taken from the station level crossing, showing the main station buildings and canopy with the signal box beyond that, in 1953. The signal box contained a 22 Saxby & Farmer lever frame, with seventeen working levers and five spares – later sixteen and six. The box remained open until the line closed in March 1967. (Stations UK) Today, the station buildings, platform and track are all gone, with a garage and shed built in their place. The common feature in both pictures is the gatepost on the extreme left. (Ray Bishop)

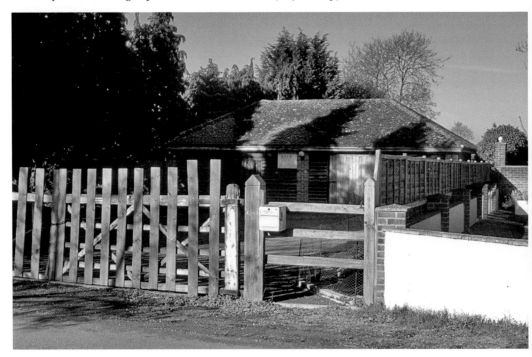

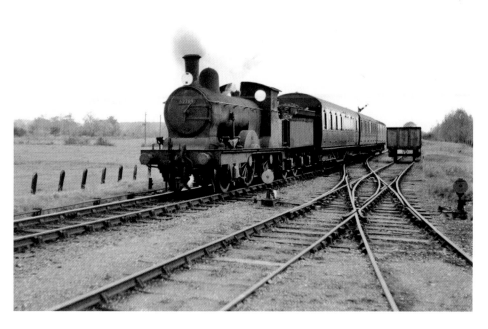

Class E4 locomotive-hauled train arriving at the station with an up local working, believed to be the 1950s. The single truck is stabled on the head shunt, awaiting the next pick up goods working. Until 1956, the up home signal, seen above the coaches, shared the same post with the down starting signal. (Dr I. C. Allen/Transport Treasury) Part of this area is now a garage, servicing cars. The road in the foreground ran behind the photographer to serve the former goods shed, now converted into apartments, which can be seen on the left of this picture. (Ray Bishop)

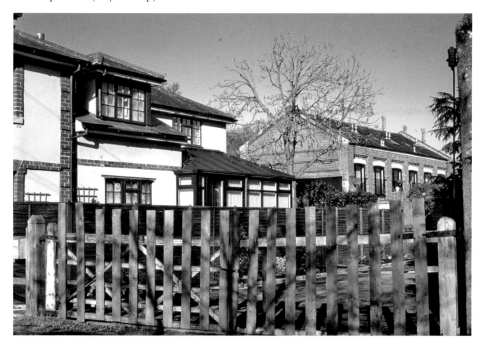

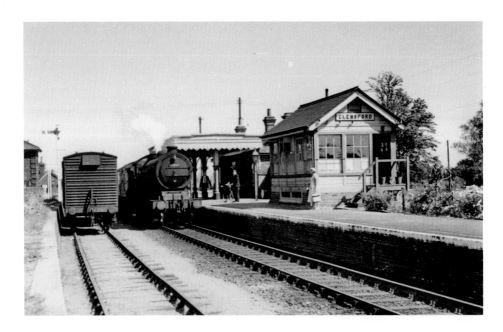

Above is a close-up view of Glemsford station building and canopy, with the signal box to the right. Although not a block post, the signal box was used every day trains ran, due to the adjacent level crossing and protecting signals. A down steam-hauled train is arriving. (Stations UK) Now all swept away, the building, canopy and signal box are no more. The track bed now forms part of the gardens, and is fenced off from the rest of the property. The two surviving railway buildings are the former crossing keeper's cottage – shown in this view, now extensively enlarged – and the former goods shed, which has been converted into apartments. (Ray Bishop)

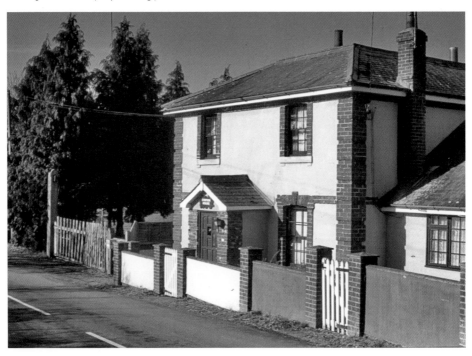

Cavendish

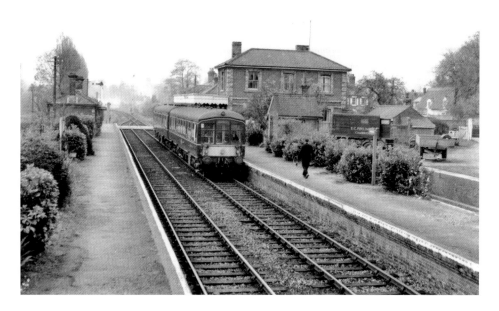

A two-car Derby Lightweight Diesel Multiple Unit (DMU) is seen arriving at the up platform at Cavendish in the early 1960s (*above*). The signalman is waiting to exchange the single line tablet with the driver for the next section, which would be from Cavendish to Long Melford. This view was taken from the signal box. (Dr I. C. Allen/Transport Treasury) Today, nothing remains at Cavendish. A housing development occupies the former station site and goods yard, and the platforms have been removed. (Ray Bishop)

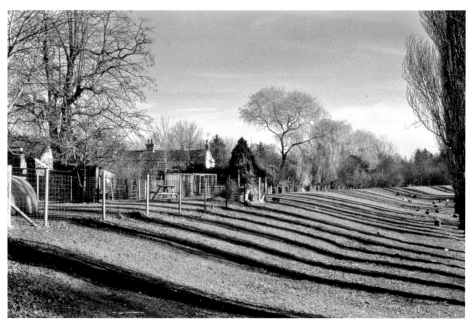

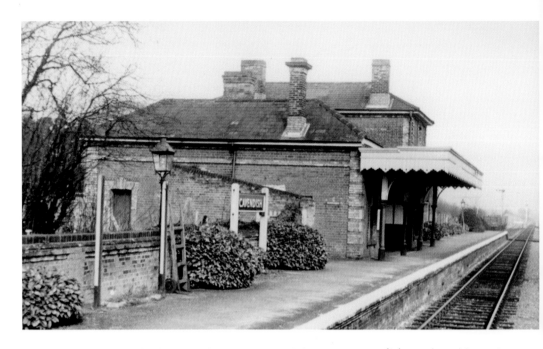

The main station buildings and Station Master's house, at Cavendish, as viewed from the level crossing looking towards Long Melford, 6 May 1955. (R. M. Casserley)

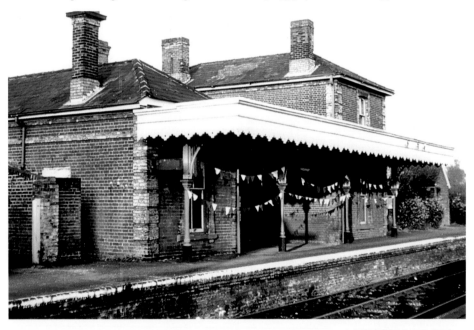

A close-up colour view, taken Sunday 5 March 1967, the day after the last trains had run. Although the station was closing, somebody put up bunting on the final day to mark the end of the train services. The station buildings and goods yard were sold for redevelopment very soon after closing, and the building was knocked down in the summer of 1967, leaving just a bare platform and rusting track. It would be another two years before the track was recovered for scrap. (Brian Pask)

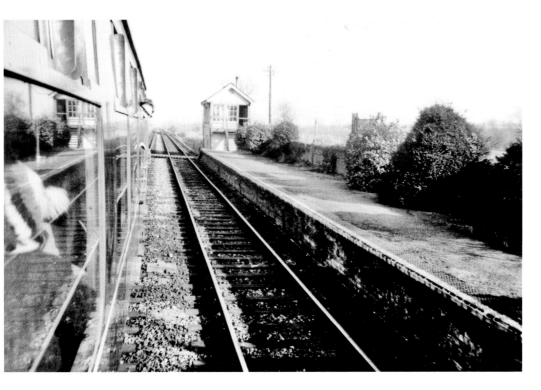

Above, Cavendish station is seen from a passing DMU, on the last day of service over this part of the line. The signal box remained in use until the end, although it had lost some functions when the adjacent goods yard closed in 1965. (Dickie Pearce) Today, the platforms and rails have all gone and some of the land has been incorporated into the gardens of the adjacent houses, which were all built on the former railway land. (Ray Bishop)

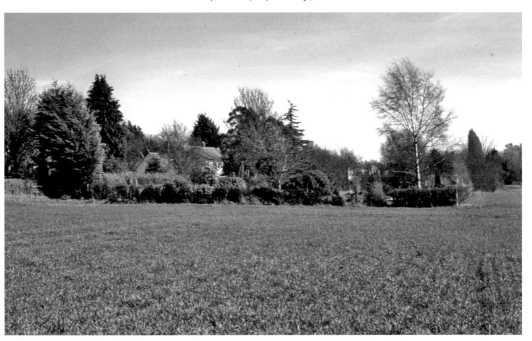

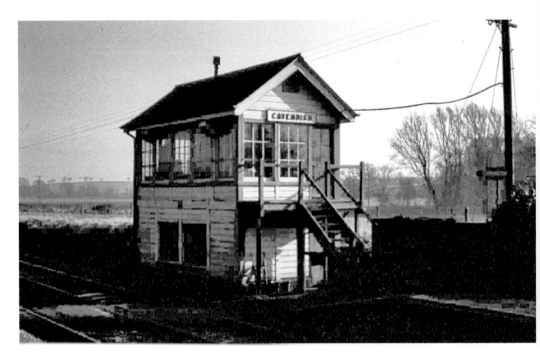

A colour view of Cavendish signal box, 18 February 1967, a couple of months before the line closed. The signal box contained a twenty-two-lever Saxby & Farmer lever frame, which had started life with seventeen working levers and five spare levers, later eighteen and four. In 1965, the goods yard closed and the box lost three more working levers. (D. J. Plyer) Today, the former station site has been totally eradicated, with little left to show that a railway once ran at this location. (Ray Bishop)

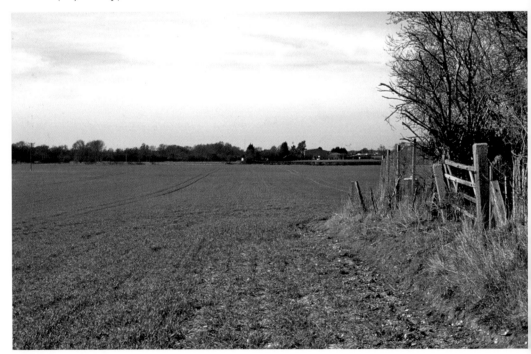

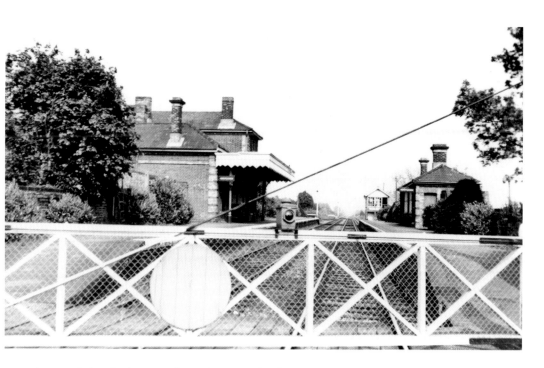

A general view looking east from the station level crossing at Cavendish. This picture features the main buildings on the up platform, including the Station Master's house, the up side buildings, and the signal box at the end of the up platform, which contained a twenty-two-lever Saxby & Farmer lever frame. The signal box was working right to the end, albeit in a reduced form. (R. M. Casserley) Today, nothing remains apart from a small piece of platform at the level crossing end. The crossing keeper's house has been turned into a private dwelling. (Ray Bishop)

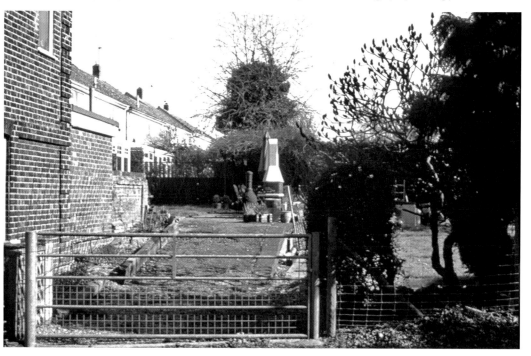

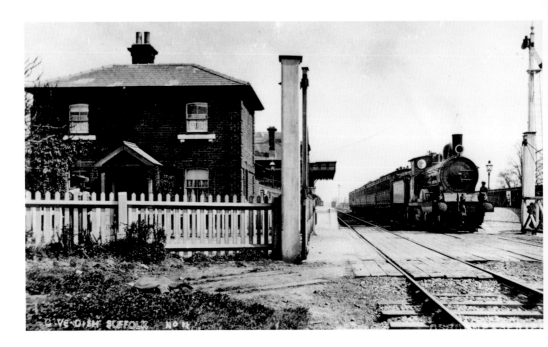

Above, a Great Eastern view of a down locomotive-hauled train arriving at Cavendish, taken from the far side of the road level crossing. The building on the left is the crossing keeper's house, which survived the demolition of the station. (Lens of Sutton Association) Today, the crossing keeper's house is a private dwelling, well screened by trees and bushes. The remainder of the station is now private housing. An alternative view, from the road looking at the level crossing: the parked car indicates the site of the level crossing. (Ray Bishop)

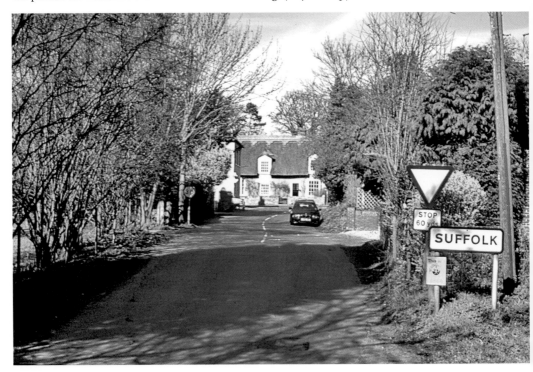

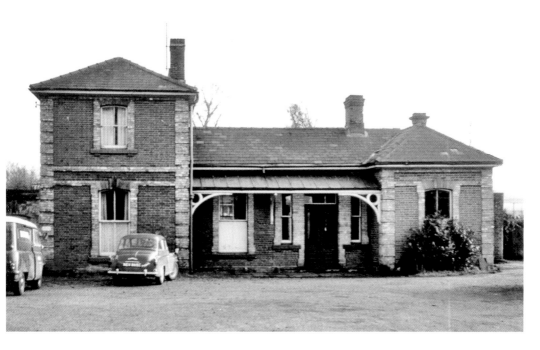

Above, a rare colour view of the exterior of Cavendish station in the 1960s. After the railway through the station closed completely, the old goods yard and station buildings were sold off for redevelopment, and the station buildings were demolished in 1967, well before the track had been lifted. (Brian Pask) Today, standing on the main road, you have a pleasant view of the houses built in 1967–68. Nothing remains of the former railway. (Ray Bishop)

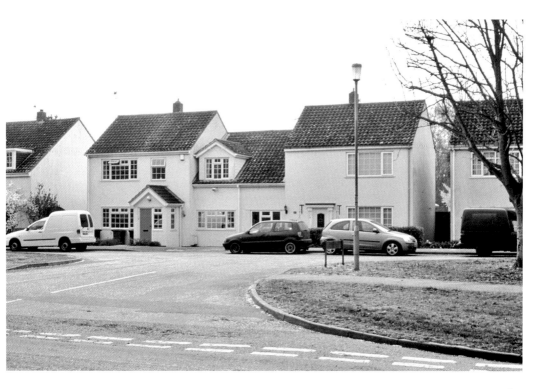

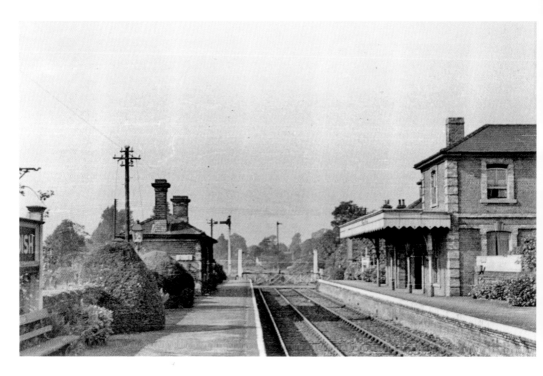

A peaceful scene, taken in 1952, when railways were still important to the transport of goods and materials, including passengers. The local staff took pride in keeping their stations neat and tidy. (Stations UK) Today, all is gone, so rather than another view of the farmer's field we have an alternate view to the one above, taken 4 March 1967 – the last day trains ran. (Stations UK)

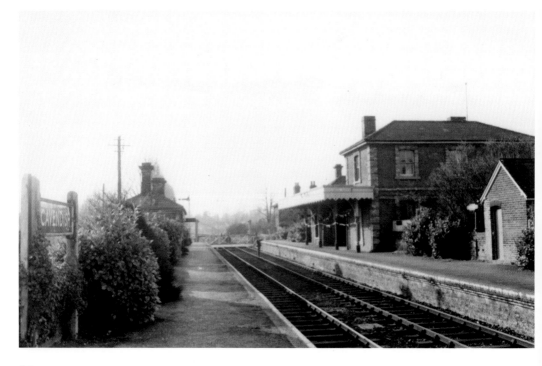

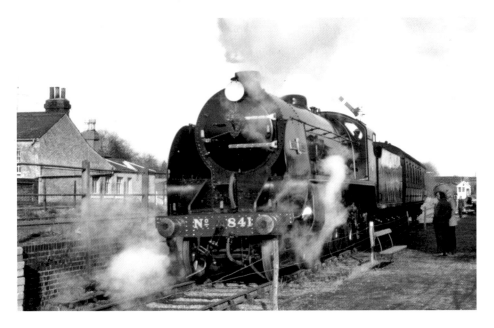

Southern S15 4-6-0 number 841 *Green King* at the then Stour Valley Railway Preservation site, at Chappel & Wakes Colne station, 11 November 1974. This locomotive arrived at Chappel and was restored to main line specification before it departed to work on the main line and to visit other railways. It is now based on the North Yorkshire Moors Railway. (Nick Ellis)

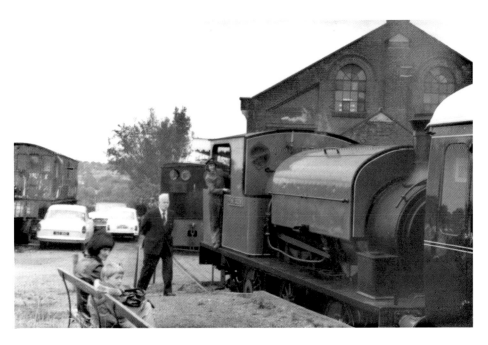

August 1978 view with *Kitson* locomotive waiting to depart from the demonstration platform. The original goods shed can be seen in the background. (Andy T. Wallis)

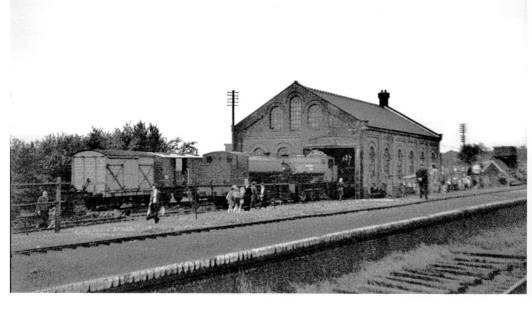

A general view of the then 'Chappel Yard' of the Stour Valley Railway. The brick-built goods shed is now used as a large function room, and hosted weddings and beer festivals in recent years. (Nick Ellis) The East Anglian Railway Museum today covers a much-enlarged site, as the view below from the footbridge shows. The original goods shed is seen in the middle of this view. (Paul Lemon)

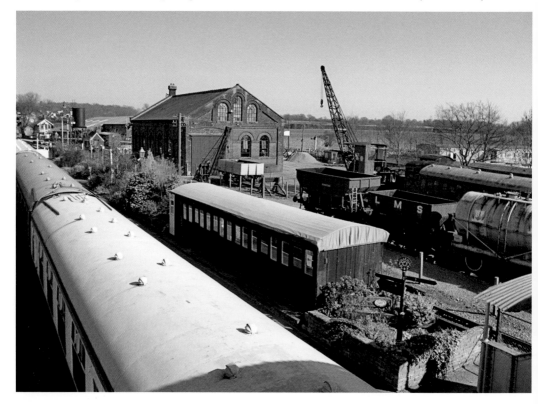

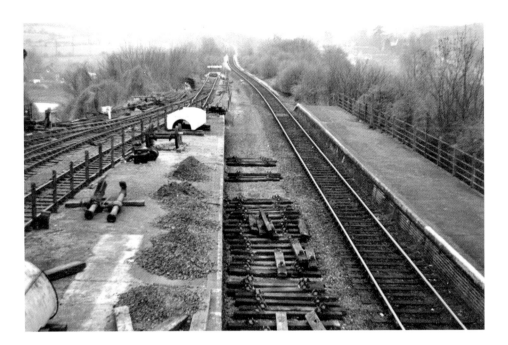

This early 1980s view, taken from the footbridge looking south, shows the track being re-laid in the former up platform at Chappel & Wakes Colne. This work was being done by the museum, who up to that time were not allowed access to this part of the track. (Andy T. Wallis) Today, with a modern digital camera you can get a view all the way over Chappel Viaduct. The track on the right is the Network Rail Sudbury branch, and the two lines ending in the buffer stops belong to the East Anglian Railway Museum. (Paul Lemon)

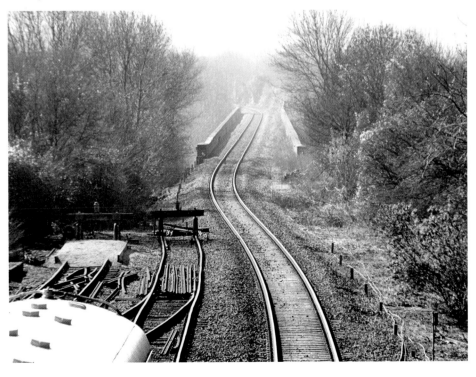

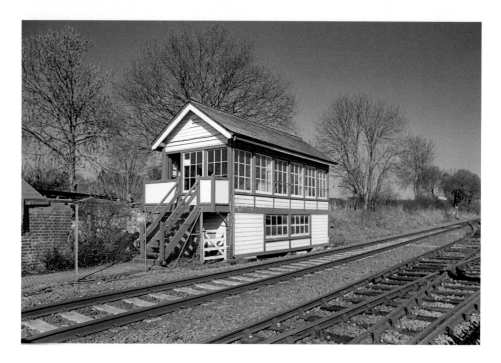

Inside and outside views of the restored Chappel Signal box. This no longer signals trains but is open to the public as part of the museum. The lever frame shown here is thirty-eight levers. During the war, it was extended to forty-two levers when an additional siding opened to serve a petroleum depot. The signal box was closed by BR in 1967. The frame was removed for scrap and was found dumped in the old yard. It was restored by museum volunteers. (Paul Lemon)

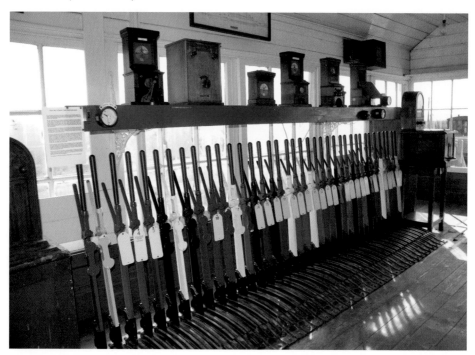

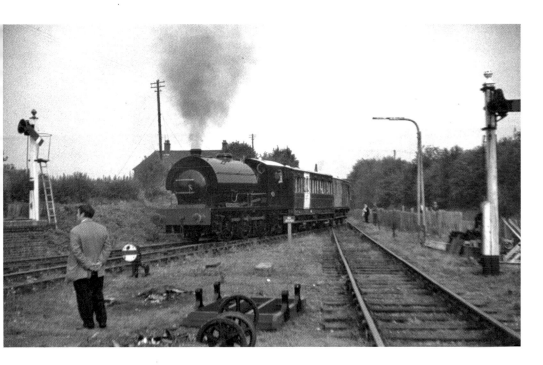

0-6-0 saddle tank *Jupiter* propels its train out of the yard platform, 15 September 1972, to give visitors a short ride up and down the yard. This view is much changed today, with the former Mistley signal box now on the end of the platform. Beyond that, the extensive workshops have been built. (Nick Ellis)

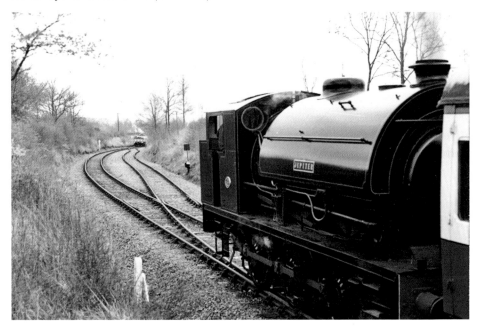

After many years of service at Chappel, *Jupiter* was sold to the nearby Colne Valley Railway, where it gave a few years service before being withdrawn for a major overhaul. In this view, we see *Jupiter* arriving at Nunnery Loop on the Colne Valley Railway. (Andy T. Wallis)

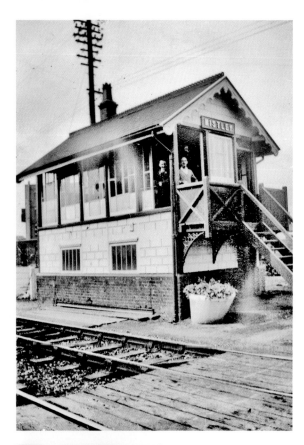

Left: The twenty-five-lever Mistley signal box on the Harwich branch, as seen in the 1950s. The signal box at Mistley was closed by BR in 1982, when the branch line to Harwich was electrified and resignalled. (Alf Foster/ CVRPS Ltd Collection)

Below: Three signal boxes. The original GER, LNER and BR Chappel & Wakes Colne signal box, the first Chappel Museum signal box, and the replacement signal, which was the former Mistley signal box on the Harwich branch. This box has found a new home at the East Anglian Railway Museum. (Andy T. Wallis)

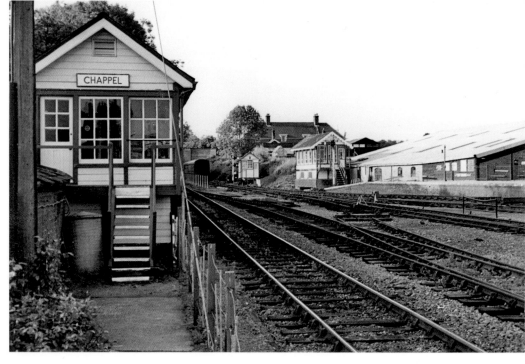

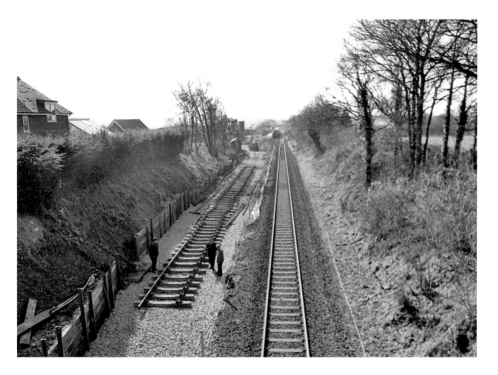

Permanent Way work on the EARM demonstration line, at Chappel & Wakes Colne station. New ballast and concrete sleepers are being laid. (Paul Lemon)

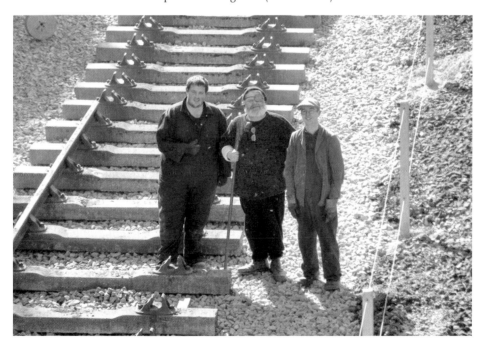

The three-man P/Way gang pose for a photograph whilst taking a break from their relaying duties. The Network Rail Sudbury branch is the line on the right. Both views are taken looking south. (Paul Lemon)

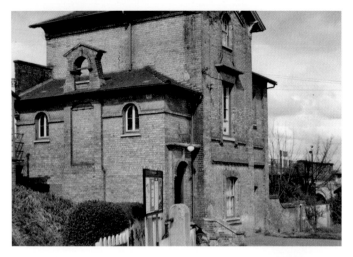

Close-up view of the original Bures Station, as built by the Colchester, Stour Valley, Sudbury & Halstead Railway back in 1849, when the original branch had opened. The buildings were demolished by British Railways in 1973, leaving a bare platform and a small waiting hut as the only shelter from the elements. (David Lawrence)

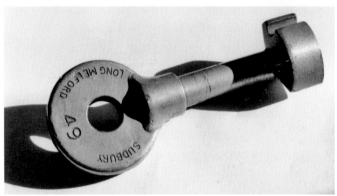

A single line key token for the Sudbury to Long Melford section, now owned by the author. A number of these tokens would be kept in two machines at either end of the section, electrically interlocked to allow only one key to be extracted at any one time.

Acknowledgements

Special thanks to Ray Bishop and Paul Lemon for the provision of the modern images, and to Brian Pask, Derek Plyer, Nick Ellis and R. M. Casserley for all their help with the archive material. Also, thanks to all the other photographers and organisations that have provided views from their collections, and special thanks to the owners of Long Melford and Welnetham stations for providing access to their properties.